# Linux headless

with PC Engines ALIX

Mathias Weidner

# Linux headless
## with PC Engines ALIX

Mathias Weidner

This book is for sale at http://www.lulu.com/

This version was published on 2013-10-19

ISBN 978-1-291-59961-9

This is a Leanpub book. Leanpub empowers authors and publishers with the Lean Publishing process. Lean Publishing is the act of publishing an in-progress ebook using lightweight tools and many iterations to get reader feedback, pivot until you have the right book and build traction once you do.

This work is licensed under a Creative Commons Attribution-ShareAlike 3.0 Unported License

# Contents

**Preface** . . . . . . . . . . . . . . . . . . . . . . . . . . . . . . 1
    Audience . . . . . . . . . . . . . . . . . . . . . . . . . . . 2
    Organization . . . . . . . . . . . . . . . . . . . . . . . . . 2
    Conventions . . . . . . . . . . . . . . . . . . . . . . . . . . 4
    Acknowledgements . . . . . . . . . . . . . . . . . . . . . . 4

**What can I do with it** . . . . . . . . . . . . . . . . . . . . 7
    Router . . . . . . . . . . . . . . . . . . . . . . . . . . . . . 7
    Firewall / packet filter . . . . . . . . . . . . . . . . . . . . 8
    Streaming client for music from the net . . . . . . . . 10
    Network information server . . . . . . . . . . . . . . . 10
    File, streaming or web server . . . . . . . . . . . . . . 11
    A weather station or something similar . . . . . . . . 11
    A controlling computer for your own hardware project 12

**Hardware for Headless Linux** . . . . . . . . . . . . . . 13
    CompactFlash card . . . . . . . . . . . . . . . . . . . . . 15
    LED . . . . . . . . . . . . . . . . . . . . . . . . . . . . . . 16
    Mode switch . . . . . . . . . . . . . . . . . . . . . . . . . 19
    Sensors . . . . . . . . . . . . . . . . . . . . . . . . . . . . 22

**Additional hardware** . . . . . . . . . . . . . . . . . . . . 25

# CONTENTS

    I²C Bus . . . . . . . . . . . . . . . . . . . . . . . . . . 25
    Serial Interface . . . . . . . . . . . . . . . . . . . . . . 27
    Sound cards . . . . . . . . . . . . . . . . . . . . . . . . 28
    UPS . . . . . . . . . . . . . . . . . . . . . . . . . . . . 28

**Suitable Linux distributions** . . . . . . . . . . . . . . . **35**
    Debian GNU/Linux . . . . . . . . . . . . . . . . . . . . . . 35
    iMedia Embedded Linux . . . . . . . . . . . . . . . . . . . 36
    OpenWrt . . . . . . . . . . . . . . . . . . . . . . . . . . 37
    Slax . . . . . . . . . . . . . . . . . . . . . . . . . . . 43
    Linux From Scratch . . . . . . . . . . . . . . . . . . . . . 44
    Buildroot . . . . . . . . . . . . . . . . . . . . . . . . . 44

**Installing Linux** . . . . . . . . . . . . . . . . . . . . . **45**
    Preparing a boot medium on a second computer . . . 45
    Installation using USB media . . . . . . . . . . . . . . 47
    Installation using PXE-Boot . . . . . . . . . . . . . . . 48

**Components of a Linux system** . . . . . . . . . . . . . . . **57**
    Kernel . . . . . . . . . . . . . . . . . . . . . . . . . . . 58
    File system . . . . . . . . . . . . . . . . . . . . . . . . 60
    Random Access Memory . . . . . . . . . . . . . . . . . . . . 68
    I/O subsystem . . . . . . . . . . . . . . . . . . . . . . . 76
    System programs . . . . . . . . . . . . . . . . . . . . . . 77
    User programs . . . . . . . . . . . . . . . . . . . . . . . 79

**Compiling software yourself** . . . . . . . . . . . . . . . . **81**
    System or user software . . . . . . . . . . . . . . . . . . 81
    Creating Debian Packages . . . . . . . . . . . . . . . . . . 83
    Kernel and kernel modules . . . . . . . . . . . . . . . . . 85
    Software for OpenWrt . . . . . . . . . . . . . . . . . . . . 87

**Daily operation and administration** . . . . . . . . . . . 89
    Configuring the computer for its intended use . . . . 89
    The iptables firewall on OpenWrt . . . . . . . . . . . 93
    Updates . . . . . . . . . . . . . . . . . . . . . . . . . 108
    Backup and Restore . . . . . . . . . . . . . . . . . . . 109

**Strategies for problem solving** . . . . . . . . . . . . . . 113
    Manual pages, program documentation . . . . . . . . 113
    Internet, search engines . . . . . . . . . . . . . . . . . 114
    Strategies for local problems on the computer . . . . . 115
    Strategies for network problems . . . . . . . . . . . . 120

**Protocols and mechanisms** . . . . . . . . . . . . . . . . 127
    Bootloader . . . . . . . . . . . . . . . . . . . . . . . . 127
    Preboot Execution Environment (PXE) . . . . . . . . 130
    udev - managing devices dynamically . . . . . . . . . 134
    DHCP . . . . . . . . . . . . . . . . . . . . . . . . . . 137
    Trivial File Transfer Protocol (TFTP) . . . . . . . . . . 142
    Zero Configuration Networking . . . . . . . . . . . . 145

**Glossary** . . . . . . . . . . . . . . . . . . . . . . . . . . 151

**Additional resources** . . . . . . . . . . . . . . . . . . . 165
    Internet . . . . . . . . . . . . . . . . . . . . . . . . . . 165
    File systems . . . . . . . . . . . . . . . . . . . . . . . 166
    ALIX hardware . . . . . . . . . . . . . . . . . . . . . 167
    Additional hardware . . . . . . . . . . . . . . . . . . 167
    Linux . . . . . . . . . . . . . . . . . . . . . . . . . . . 168
    Literature . . . . . . . . . . . . . . . . . . . . . . . . 172
    RFC - Requests for Comment . . . . . . . . . . . . . 172

**Colophon** . . . . . . . . . . . . . . . . . . . . . . . . . 177

# Preface

I have noticed that every personal computer costs - first and foremost - time. It doesn't matter whether it runs on MS Windows, OSX, Linux or UNIX, how much time it saves me or what - formerly unknown - possibilities it opens up. It takes time for the computer to boot up, time for me to log in, time to start a program. Or - even worse - time for finding something on the internet and copying it onto my computer. The PC can do nearly anything - allows me do nearly anything. But it also takes up my time and distracts me - because, while waiting for one thing, I can do this or that. Pretty soon I'm in multitasking mode and getting next to nothing done.

But this book is about something else. It's about small computers, built for one purpose: to be switched on and soon forgotten. It's about computers that don't have a keyboard or a display, that are there to do what they were built for. Sure such a device is boring when it works. But this book is not about using such devices, it is about building one.

- What do I need to do this?
- What do I have to consider?
- What can I do with such a device?
- What must I know in order to build it?
- What is already there?
- What kind of hardware can I use?

Certainly many things in this book will be outdated in short time, given the pace with which information technology evolves. Therefore I'll try to carve out some fundamental principals and take the available hardware as an example.

## Audience

This book is for anyone who wants to build their individual computer according to their own design based on PC Engine ALIX or similar hardware.

It presumes a basic knowledge of the UNIX command line.

To build the UPS circuit, basic knowledge about electronics assembly is required.

## Organization

The **first part** of the book deals with the things I can do or want to do with such a device. What software do I need and what special things do I need to consider? Problems will be dealt with in more detail in later chapters.

Chapter one illustrates some applications and talks about some basic conditions for these applications. These may include the number of interfaces for a networking device, additional hardware for special purposes or particular software requirements.

The **second part** deals with the hardware used. What does it have in common with personal computers, what is different?

Chapter two goes into detail about PC Engines ALIX computers. What hardware options are there? Which device drivers do I need? What software is available especially for this hardware?

Chapter three covers additional hardware for special projects.

The **third part** deals with the software used. It is about appropriate Linux distributions and how to install them onto the hardware. It also explains about the components of a Linux system and their purpose and about additional software and how to install it onto the system.

Chapter four goes into some Linux distributions that I find suitable for headless Linux projects.

Chapter five illustrates different ways of installing my choice of Linux distribution into the hardware.

Chapter six goes into detail about the components of a Linux system. What is their purpose and what alternatives do I have?

Chapter seven shows how I can compile and install software that is not available in my chosen Linux distribution.

The **fourth part** of the book deals with the daily operation and offers hints on how to solve possible problems.

Chapter eight goes into detail about daily operation. How do I configure the device for the operational environment? How do I update the system? How do I know if security updates are needed in the first place?

Chapter nine presents some trouble-shooting strategies. What can I do if a program doesn't start at all? When it crashes? How do I track problems in the network? Which programs help me with which problems?

Chapter ten introduces some protocols and mechanisms that I may encounter in the course of the project which may prove helpful to know about.

Chapter eleven lists some additional resources that may provide help for some problems.

## Conventions

Program code and input in the command line is written in `constant width` text. This is also used inside paragraphs for literal command line options.

Emphasized text is written in *italics*.

## Acknowledgements

This book began as accompanying documentation for a few projects with PC Engine ALIX computers.

I would like to thank the users of the PC Engines support forum for their helpful suggestions, especially Nicolas (*pure_debian*) for his reference to *flashybrid* and for the idea of using virtual machines.

Willy Tarreau suggested I use the PC8591 to monitor the mini UPS which made the circuit considerably easier.

Thanks go to KDG Wittenberg for providing me with some ALIX machines for testing purposes after my own device became operational and could only be used for a limited number of tests.

Many thanks to Lorri King from able Sprachschule for correcting my perception of how a meaningful english sentence should look. I take the credit for any remaining mistakes in English grammar and orthography.

# What can I do with it

Before I go into depth about creating a small headless Linux computer, I'd like to offer some thoughts about what one can do with such a device. This list is by no means complete and you, the reader, may have your own thoughts about where you are itching to get startet.

## Router

My first thought was to use the device to create a router (in fact this was the first device that I built). Now there is a great number of routers out there - specifically for use at home or in small offices. Many of these already come with Linux and everything else the heart desires - including a WLAN access point. What, then, would be the point of yet another router? To top it off, I would have to buy the WLAN module separately.

One advantage is the flexibility. I can buy a device with one, two or three ethernet interfaces, depending on the application, and build a router that is tailored exactly to my needs. But wait, you might think, why would I want a router with just one interface? Now there is the option of using such a device to retrospectively set up an additional transition to the new IPv6 protocal via a suitable tunnel provider in an old IPv4 network. Or I can connect to another network via VPN and use this device as a VPN router. The point behind a router with two interfaces is obvious. With three interfaces I can build a poor mans DMZ without having to resort to two devices like I had to with SOHO routers.

Well that covers flexibility. What else? Another advantage, that applies to other projects as well, is that I don't need to cross compile the software. Instead I can mostly use the software packages that come with my chosen Linux distribution. That saves tremendous time when I only want to try out something. I can directly use software in the repositories of my distribution or install software on the router that was compiled for a PC. At the same time I receive the security updates of my distribution.

In the end I have such a vast amount of software at my disposal that I can diagnore or monitor anything I want in my networks within the limits of the interface transfer rate of 100 mbit/s which is usually sufficient for most WAN connections.

A router with ALIX can be left running and be switched off at any time. Since there are no moving parts (fan or hard disk) necessary to run it, there is little risk that it will fail - at least in this regard.

## Firewall / packet filter

A network firewall, or packet filter, is closely related to a router and is another example of an application.

Why, you may ask, would I risk securing my network with a handmade firewall when I can get certified firewalls from experts in this field which are good value for money and include support if I have problems and training if I need it. The simple answer is: nobody is making you. With issues of security as with all other matters everyone should weigh the pros and cons for themselves and make their own decisions.

So what are the arguments in favor of a home-made firewall? First and foremost, you need to have the necessary expertise or at least this should be acquired during the project. This knowledge includes understanding the tasks of a firewall and the way a firewall works, as well as the possibilities and constraints of a Linux system. Then there is the size of the risk that has to be considered. If the value of the network and the data that you want to protect is less than the price of a commercial firewall, this could be a point in favor of building it yourself. Finally if I only want to place an additional and/or temporary packet filter in the network a self built device may be better - especially if I already have the necessary knowledge required to do this.

What else do I need for a firewall? First I need a device with two or, better, three network interfaces. With three interfaces I can use two for the production networks and the third for administration. This way the firewall cannot be manipulated from the production networks.

For software I need *iptables* for the configuration of the filter tables and *ebtables* if I want to use the packet filter as a (layer 2) bridge instead of a (layer 3) router. Finally, I need suitable software to manage the firewall rules (I like *ferm* for this but you might have other preferences). If the firewall is to function as an VPN gateway, I need the appropriate software (*openvpn*, *strongswan*, etc).

It makes sense to have a device in the network where I can send log messages to monitor the firewall.

## Streaming client for music from the net

Voyage Linux, itself derived from Debian GNU/Linux has a variant called Voyage MPD that is dedicated to this topic.

What else do I need for this? I need a Linux-supported soundcard and an infrared sensor for the remote control. I also need a mini keyboard to operate directly at the device and a small LCD display. I could connect a hard disk and play the music off it or I could get everything off from a server. I could build the box myself or have it made according to my specifications. one possibility would be to use an old sound system for the housing.

## Network information server

What exactly is this, you may ask? It's used as follows: When I want to connect a computer to a network it's not enough to just plug a cable into an ethernet socket. The computer must know the following information in order to communicate with other computers on the local network or internet:

- Which addresses are valid in the local net and which off these can it use?
- What are the addresses of the gateways to other networks?
- What are the addresses of the nameservers that it can use?
- Where can it get the current time?
- And perhaps: where can it get its operating system?

Part of this information may be configured automatically with IPv6. IPv4 does have similar solutions now with Bonjour and Zero Configuration Networking. I use DHCP servers if I want more controle over the network. These should be some of the first devices switched on in the network and the last devices switched off. It's an ideal job for such a small permanently running device. I could also install a time service (NTP) and, while I'm at it, the name service (DNS), too. If I want to provide system images to boot other computers from, I would probably need an additional hard disk.

## File, streaming or web server

Whether I would really want to run this from a small headless computer depends on the application. I would definitely need to test whether its performance is sufficient. If it is, I could plug in one or multiple hard disks and keep the operating system on the CF card.

## A weather station or something similar

This depends on the device which I'm compiling the data from. Most have a serial or USB interface. I might need a USB serial converter.

If I want to read data continuously, I'll want to store the data somewhere. Because I really want to avoid constantly writing on the flash memory, I could use an external hard disk or some storage device in the network. Both of these may suddenly disappear, so I have make provisions for this case. It would be possible to connect an internal hard disk and use this as permanent storage.

## A controlling computer for your own hardware project

The project dictates what additional hardware and software I need.

With the I²C bus I can directly control some circuits, for instance the PCF8574 with eight digital input and output lines, or the PCF8591 with four 8-bit A/D converters and one D/A converter.

# Hardware for Headless Linux

In this book I'll concentrate on PC Engines' ALIX series of system boards. In principle most of the information here may be transferred to other hardware. I am limiting myself to this hardware because I have the most experience with these devices. I have tested nearly everything I have written here on these little machines.

Like the boards from Soekris, the ALIX boards are available as single board computer without moving parts. As long as I don't install any moving parts (like harddisks) on the devices, I can eliminate mechanical wear (provided that the device itself does not get moved and is not attached to a car or anything similar).

The advantages of these devices are that they don't require much power and are compatible with personal computers. I can choose from boards with up to three Ethernet interfaces for my project. The operating system fits onto a CompactFlash card (socket is on board) or onto a notebook harddisk that can also be connected to some of the boards. In principle I could load the operating system everytime from the network. Some of the boards have a Mini-PCI slot for expansion cards.

Most of these boards don't have a video card or a port for a keyboard but they do have a serial connection. Even the BIOS is accessible through this serial console. Only a few models have VGA and PS/2 connections.

> **Tip**
>
> I usually use *PuTTY* on computers with MS Windows to access the serial console. This program allows me to set up the connection type in the configuration menu. If I choose *serial*, I can set the interface and the baud rate. There are more options under the category *Connection/Serial*.
>
> I do have a larger selection on computers with Linux. I can also take *PuTTY* if I have a graphical desktop. Some of the programs I am able to use in an ASCII terminal include *C-Kermit*, *Minicom* and *Picocom* wich have quite a few setting options.
>
> If I have not installed any of these programs before, I can use *screen*. This program is installed on nearly all of my Linux computers. With *screen* I can access a serial interface like this:
>
> ```
> $ screen /dev/ttyS0 38400
> ```
>
> or (without flow control):
>
> ```
> $ screen /dev/ttyS0 38400,-ixon,-ixoff
> ```

There are also USB interfaces on the board. The boards without VGA have TinyBIOS in the flash ROM which allows for a few configuration options.

> **Tip**
>
> Press s during the memory test to enter setup in TinyBIOS. The operating manual describes the options available. It can be found at the webpage of PC Engines[a].
>
> ---
> [a] http://pcengines.ch

If I don't plan to use a special housing for my project, I can usually find the right case where I buy the boards.

## CompactFlash card

The boards of the ALIX.2 and the ALIX.6 series do have CompactFlash adapters so that you can put the operating system and the data on a CF card. That way the whole system remains compact and is less sensitive to mechanical wear and tear.

To extend the lifetime of the CF card I minimize the writing access by setting it to read-only. Alternatively I can use the TRIM command, which has been available since CompactFlash 5.0 came out, and a sufficient new Linux (with a kernel version of at least 2.6.33) as well as an appropriate file system (*btrfs*, *ext4fs*, *fat*, *gfs2*). These file systems may use the TRIM command to help with the wear leveling of the CF firmware.

## LED

There are three LED on the boards that are visible through the case. I can use two kernel modules to control these LEDs: the *leds_alix2* module and the *cs5535_gpio* module which can directly drive the pins of the GPIO chip CS5535. With kernel versions >= 2.6.33, I have to make sure that only one LED module loads. This can be done, for instance, through blacklisting in */etc/modprobe.d/blacklist*:

```
blacklist cs5535_gpio
```

The LED module provides access to the LEDs via *sysfs*. To switch them on or off I use the file *brightness*:

```
# echo 1 > /sys/class/leds/alix\:3/brightness
# sleep 5
# echo 0 > /sys/class/leds/alix\:3/brightness
```

Using these three commands I was able to switch on the third LED and after five seconds switch it off again.

Additionally there are trigger modules that support some applications. I will introduce a few of them in a moment, but first lets look at the *heartbeat* trigger:

```
# modprobe ledtrig-heartbeat
# echo heartbeat > /sys/class/leds/alix\:2/trigger
```

This allows me to put a predetermined pulse pattern on an LED (in this case the second LED).

Next there is the *timer* trigger:

```
# modprobe ledtrig-timer
# echo timer > /sys/class/leds/alix\:1/trigger
# echo 1000 > /sys/class/leds/alix\:1/delay_on
# echo 100 > /sys/class/leds/alix\:1/delay_off
```

In this example the first LED switches on for 1000 ms and then switches off for 100 ms repetitively.

To monitor the activity of IDE disks I can use the trigger *ide-disk*. I don't need to load an extra kernel module to do this.

```
# echo ide-disk > /sys/class/leds/alix\:2/trigger
```

If I'm in the mood, I can emit Morse code signals with the LEDs:

```
# modprobe ledtrig-morse
# echo morse > /sys/class/leds/alix\:1/trigger
# echo "SOS" > /sys/class/leds/alix\:1/message
# echo 100 > /sys/class/leds/alix\:1/delay
```

I set the speed of the Morse code with the value that I enter under *delay*.

The *netdev* trigger is even more useful by allowing me to monitor network activity.

```
# modprobe ledtrig-netdev
# echo netdev > /sys/class/leds/alix\:2/trigger
# echo ppp0 > /sys/class/leds/alix\:2/device_name
# echo link tx rx > /sys/class/leds/alix\:2/mode
```

In this example the second LED switches on as soon as a PPP connection is established and blinks if there is any traffic going over this connection.

I can find out which triggers are momentarily available and active by reading the file *trigger*:

```
# cat /sys/class/leds/alix\:1/trigger
```
none ide-disk [morse] default-on gpio heartbeat \
netdev timer usbdev
```
# cat /sys/class/leds/alix\:2/trigger
```
none ide-disk morse default-on gpio heartbeat \
[netdev] timer usbdev

I deactivate the triggers by writing none in this file.

```
# echo none > /sys/class/leds/alix\:1/trigger
# echo none > /sys/class/leds/alix\:2/trigger
# echo none > /sys/class/leds/alix\:3/trigger
```

> **Tip**
>
> With ALIX 3D3 boards, LEDs may not be recognized from the kernel module *leds-alix2*. One reason could be that there is another BIOS on this board as there is on the ALIX

2.x devices. In this case, entering `leds-alix2.force=1` as a kernel boot parameter may help. Otherwise the loading of the kernel module is aborted with the message `FATAL: Error inserting leds_alix2 (.../leds-alix2.ko): No such device`.

## Mode switch

There is a little switch on the ALIX boards that helps you enter the BIOS setup at system start if the serial interface has been deactivated. This switch is connected to pin 24 of the GPIO chip CS5536 and may be queried if kernel support for this chip is activated. Alternatively one can query bit 8 at I/O port 0x61b0. 0 signifies a pressed switch.

### Kernel module

I can use the kernel module *css5535-gpio* with the kernel of Voyage Linux 0.7. In doing so I have to keep in mind possible problems with the kernel module *leds-alix*:

```
# modprobe cs5535-gpio
# ls -l /sys/class/gpio/
total 0
--w------- 1 root root 4096 Dec  7 07:24 export
--w------- 1 root root 4096 Dec  7 07:25 unexport
# echo 24 > /sys/class/gpio/export
# ls -l /sys/class/gpio/GPIO24/
total 0
-rw-r--r-- 1 root root 4096 Dec  7 07:31 active_low
-rw-r--r-- 1 root root 4096 Dec  7 07:31 direction
drwxr-xr-x 2 root root    0 Dec  7 07:31 power
lrwxrwxrwx 1 root root    0 Dec  7 07:31 subsystem \
-> ../../../../class/gpio
-rw-r--r-- 1 root root 4096 Dec  7 07:31 uevent
-rw-r--r-- 1 root root 4096 Dec  7 07:31 value
# echo in > /sys/class/gpio/GPIO24/direction
# cat /sys/class/gpio/GPIO24/value
1
# echo 24 > /sys/class/gpio/unexport
```

Initially the directory */sys/class/gpio/* only contains the files *export* and *unexport*. Here I enter the number of the pin that I want to use. For the mode switch this is pin 24. After I enter this number in the file *export*, the kernel module opens up more pseudo files in the directory */sys/class/gpio/GPIO24/* to control and query the pin. At this point in time I'm only interested in the file *direction*, which determines whether I want to use the pin as input or output, and in the file *value* which allows me to read the value.

## Query the I/O port

As an alternative to the kernel module I can directly read the I/O port through which the switch can be accessed. This can be done, for instance, using the following small C program:

mode-switch.c

```
/* mode-switch.c - access mode-switch from ALIX Boards
 *
 * Exit value 0 means switch is pressed.
 */

#include <sys/io.h>
#include <stdio.h>
#include <stdlib.h>

#define MSPORT 0x61b0
#define MSMASK 0x100

int main() {
        if (ioperm(MSPORT,2,1)) {
                perror("ioperm");
                exit(255);
        }
        int status = 0 == (inw(MSPORT) & MSMASK);
        exit(status ? 0 : 1);
}
```

I compile the program like this:

```
$ gcc -O2 mode-switch.c -o mode-switch -m32
```

The option -m32 is important if I'm compiling the program on a 64-bit-system. Then I also need the package libc6-dev-i386 that contains some required header files.

For instance, to synchronize the system status with a keypress, I can use the above program to periodically query the state of the switch in an endless loop and backup the temporary data when the key is pressed:

```
1  while true; do
2    if /root/bin/mode-switch ; then
3      /etc/init.d/voyage-sync sync
4      sleep 60
5    else
6      sleep 1
7    fi
8  done
```

In this script the state of the switch is queried every second. This means I have to hold down the switch for somewhat more than a second to be sure that it is recognized. Once the keypress is recognized, the synchronization script is called up and the switch isn't queried the next time for at least 60 seconds. Of course I could use one of the LEDs to signalize that the keypress was recognized.

## Sensors

In order to query the sensors on the board, I can install the software package *lm-sensors*.

The kernel modules required are *scx200_acb* for the I²C controller and *lm90* for the temperature sensors that are connected to the I²C bus.

I can query the sensors using the command sensors:

```
$ sensors
lm86-i2c-0-4c
Adapter: CS5536 ACB0
temp1:        +38.0 C (low  =  +0.0 C, high = +70.0 C)
                      (crit = +85.0 C, hyst = +75.0 C)
temp2:        +44.0 C (low  =  +0.0 C, high = +70.0 C)
                      (crit = +85.0 C, hyst = +75.0 C)
```

*temp1* gives me a temperature reading of the main board and *temp2* gives me a temperature reading of the processor.

# Additional hardware

I can do quite a lot with the machines described in the previous chapter an for most projects I don't need any further hardware. But sometimes things won't work without additional hardware at the peripherals. This chapter will offer you a few tips.

## I²C Bus

The pins of the I²2 bus are led through *J8* (ALIX.3) and *J13* respectively (ALIX.2, ALIX.6). I may have to solder on a pin header depending on the assembly of the board. Using this connection it is possible to attach further circuits which are accessible by the I²C bus. I²C tools (software package i2c-tools from Debian) helps to setup these circuits. If necessary I can look up in the kernel documentation to find out which sensors are already supported by the kernel.

The kernel's interface is one simple way to work with the I²C bus. I access this interface by loading the kernel module *i2c-dev*.

```
# modprobe i2c-dev
```

After loading the module, a device file is often automatically created under */dev/* for each I²C bus of the machine. On ALIX boards */dev/i2c-0*, this is only done for the first and only bus. If the device file isn't created automatically I can do this manually using the command *mknod*:

# Additional hardware

```
# mknod /dev/i2c-0 c 89 0
```

With the command *i2cdetect* I can verify whether a circuit has been detected on the I²C bus. A PCF8591, with all address bits set to 0 should appear at address 48 hex:

```
# i2cdetect -y 0
     0  1  2  3  4  5  6  7  8  9  a  b  c  d  e  f
00:          -- -- -- -- -- -- -- -- -- -- -- -- --
10: -- -- -- -- -- -- -- -- -- -- -- -- -- -- -- --
...
40: -- -- -- -- -- -- -- -- 48 -- -- -- 4c -- -- --
...
```

I use the programs *i2cset* and *i2cget* to send and read data via the I²C Bus. This allows me, for example, to query the values at the four analog inputs of a PCF8591as follows:

```
# i2cget 0 0x48 0x40
0x80
# i2cget 0 0x48 0x41
0xff
# i2cget 0 0x48 0x42
0x20
# i2cget 0 0x48 0x43
0x00
# i2cget 0 0x48 0x40
0x73
```

With this circuit I need to remember that it provides the value for the control word (0x40..0x43) of the previous query in the next query. You will find more information about this in the circuit's datasheet; the corresponding manual pages will help you with the programs.

## Serial Interface

With a little bit of soldering I may be able to use an additional serial port directly on the board. The ALIX 2D13 model has a second serial interface at connector *J12* with a 3.3V CMOS signal level which I can convert with the right converter.

If I don't want to get my hands dirty or don't want to burn my fingers (for lack of soldering skills) I can always use USB-to-serial converters. Here the problem sometimes arises that the converter gets reset when connecting or disconnecting the serial interface and a new name is given by the kernel (for instance *ttyUSB1* instead of *ttyUSB0*). Thus programs which use the serial interface may get mixed up. I have to use appropriate *udev* rules to counteract this.

> **Tipp**
>
> If I know that I always want to use exactly one USB-to-serial converter, I can create a link to the device with the following rule in */etc/udev/rules.d/usb-serial.rules*:
>
> ```
> 1  SUBSYSTEMS=="usb-serial", SYMLINK+="usb-serial"
> ```
>
> More tips to *udev* are in the chapter Protocols and mechanisms.

## Sound cards

Here I can use USB sound cards. According to their homepage, any sound devices that support a standard USB Audio Class 2.0 (UAC2) interface will work with *Voyage Linux MPD*. Alternatively I may use the onboard audio device that comes with the ALIX.1d or ALIX.3d3 devices.

## UPS

Willy Tarreau wrote a web article about how to build a cheap UPS with very few components that could sustain an ALIX computer for about ten minutes. That's not a lot of time to save the world but at my home the power fails a few times a year long enough to shut off all computers without UPS or battery (notebooks). And for those short blackouts 10 minutes are more than enough. You can also use it to plug the power supply into another socket without having to restart the system.

There is just one small problem with this UPS: after these ten minutes the power fails just as it would have done without the UPS. So if I want to use the time gained by the UPS for something important, such as saving some important files from memory to disk, the system has to know when it is running on battery.

Fortunately with a few resistors and a PCF8591 circuit I can augment the circuit so that the system can query the state of the power supply via I$^2$C bus and - after some test runs - make some predictions about the remaining battery time. This makes this cheap UPS suitable for a broader scope of applications.

## The circuit

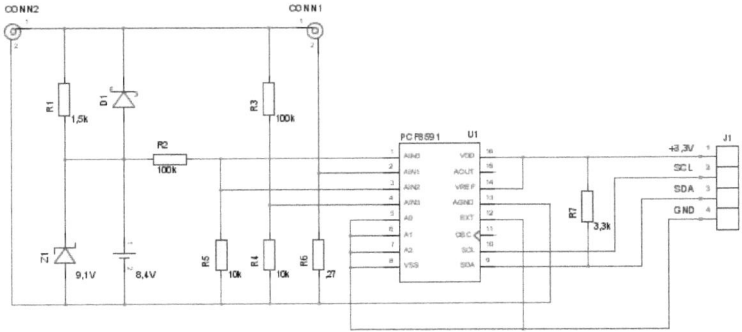

USV with monitoring extension

Willy Tarreau's original circuit consists of a rechargeable 8.4V battery, a current-limiting resistor R1, a Zener diode Z1, which limits the charging voltage for the battery and a low voltage Schottky diode D1 which conducts the current from the battery to the ALIX board if there is a power outage.

The extension that makes it possible to query the state of the UPS consists of voltage dividers R5/R2 and R4/R3 as well as a resistor R6 which works as a measuring current transformer. These prepare the voltage level and the total current in such a way that they can be processed at the analog inputs of the PCF8591. Resistor R7 pulls the I²C data bus (line *SDA*) to VCC because the output lines of the circuit only pull it to GND.

## Notes on dimensions

R1 limits the charging current for the battery. The 18V from the power supply unit reduced by 8.4V nominal voltage from the battery makes about 9.6V. Willy Tarreau recommends values between 820 and 1500 ohms. This would make the charging current 12 to 6 mA. If there is a short in the battery poles an 820 ohm resistor must dissipate about 400 mW. With 1500 ohms it is still 220 mW and the resistor must sustain this dissipation loss.

The Zener diode Z1 takes the charging current once the voltage of the battery reaches the avalanche voltage. Willy Tarreau specified a voltage of 9.6V in his circuit. I had only 9.1V diodes at my disposal. The voltage can be expanded with an additional diode connected in series. With 820 ohms for R1, the current through Z1 is about 10 mA which leads to about 100 mW of heat that has to be dissipated. With 1500 ohms for R1 it is less than 65 mW.

The Schottky diode has to continuously support the full current of the ALIX board should power fail. According to the specification, peak power is 6 watts and the device runs on at least 7 volt. That means this diode has to support at least 1A of continuous current.

According to Willy Tarreau's article, an 8.4V battery keeps the ALIX board online for about 10 minutes until the voltage drops below 7 volts. Around 24 hours are required for a complete charge with a 1500 ohm resistor.

To dimension the monitoring circuit with the PCF8591 I will briefly touch upon the wiring. The A/D converters compare the analog input voltage with the voltage reference (VREF) in 256 steps (8 bit). Accordingly they should not be above the voltage reference (VREF) and not below the analog ground (AGND).

VREF comes from the I²C port of the ALIX board and is 3.3V with reference to the VSS. The VSS is the ground wire of the ALIX board at the hot end of R6. This means that the analog voltage reference is 3.3V plus the potential difference in R6 (it floats a bit depending on the current taken by the ALIX board). With a minimum voltage of 7 volts and 6 watt power loss, the maximum current through R6 is less than 1 ampere.

To keep the potential difference in R6 low, I chose 0.27 ohms for this resistor. Thus the maximum difference is less than 0.3 volts and the voltage reference for the A/D converters is between 3.3 and 3.6 volts. This voltage, divided by 256, gives a precision in the A/D converters of between 13 and 14 mV per digit. This equates to a current of 48 to 52 mA per digit on the 0.27 ohm resistor. This is the precision with which I can estimate the voltage and the current.

With a total of one ampere I can use a resistor with a maximum thermal dissipation of half a watt.

Because the input voltage from the power supply is a maximum of 20 volt and the voltage reference is between 3.3 and 3.6 volt, the ratio of R5 to R2 and R4 to R3 should not exceed one sixth. I am on the safe side with a ratio of 1 to 10. Using the precision of the voltage reference I can estimate that the power input and the battery power is 0.13 to 0.14 volts per digit.

## Querying the state of the UPS

I use the analog inputs AIN0 and AIN1 in the circuit to query the absolute values of the battery voltage and the total current. The inputs AIN2 and AIN3 are queried as a difference value. This way I only need to observe the polarity of this value to know whether the board is running on battery or power supply.

The way the inputs are connected, I obtain with the control bytes

- *0x60* the battery voltage
- *0x61* the total current
- *0x62* the polarity and the voltage in R1 and D1. Here the most significant bit (MSB) is enough to determine if the board is running on battery or not.

Alternatively I can obtain with the control bytes

- *0x40* or *0x42* the battery voltage
- *0x41* the total current
- *0x43* the output voltage, that is fed into the ALIX board.

Then I have to subtract the battery voltage from the output voltage to determine whether it is running on battery or not. Because I need two query cycles it is better to first query the battery voltage. (If the power fails between these two queries, the battery voltage would still appear to be less than the output voltage and that would mean the board is fueled by the power grid).

I made a test set-up with a power supply of 12 volts and obtained the following readings.

```
# i2cget -y 0 0x48 0x60
0x80

# i2cget -y 0 0x48 0x61
0x3e
# i2cget -y 0 0x48 0x62
0x07
# i2cget -y 0 0x48 0x60
0xdc
```

And with the power supply switched off:

```
# i2cget -y 0 0x48 0x61
0x3d
# i2cget -y 0 0x48 0x62
0x0c
# i2cget -y 0 0x48 0x60
0x01
```

Here the third value stands out because its sign changes (negative when on power supply, positive when on battery) and because its absolute value changes (charging voltage difference in R1 versus flux voltage of D1). Furthermore the current drain is higher when the battery in order to compensate for the lower voltage.

# Suitable Linux distributions

In this chapter I will look at Linux distributions that are, in my opinion, particularly suitable for the X86 embedded platform. Of course this view is completely subjective since my experience extends to a relatively few number of distributions. In the end, nearly every distribution is probably suitable: one makes it easier, the other harder to adapt to this platform. One hint when choosing your distribution is to look at the minimum requirements needed to install it. If anything, the minimum RAM and hard disk space requirements are usually specified. These, along with a certain reserve for extra software should match the specs of the machine.

If you do have some experience with a distribution - and it is basically suitable - it might be a good idea to use this as a starting point. Sometimes there are projects, that prepare a distribution for an intended use.

## Debian GNU/Linux

In the past few years I have gained experience with Debian GNU/Linux and some distributions derived from this. On my first ALIX machine I installed *Debian 6 Squeeze* with the installer which came with the distribution. I had mounted the file system completely read-only and used AUFS to allow processes to write things on the disk. This is one possibility, though perhaps not the smartest when it comes to administration and updates. A better solution would be to put the directories with write access on a *tmpfs*. This can be achieved with the software package *flashybrid*.

## Voyage Linux

A little bit later I discovered *Voyage Linux*. This distribution is derived from Debian and works best on platforms like PC Engines ALIX or WRAP, Soekris 45xx/48xx and boards with an ATOM processor. Most of the software is directly from Debian so that I can use the Debian servers as the source for software packages. Only a few additional packages are needed which provide support for the devices and the organization of the file systems.

Currently Voyage Linux has two editions:

- **Voyage Linux** - the basic version
- **Voyage MPD** - Music Player Daemon

All of the editions come as a distribution tarball and as a Live CD in i386 architecture. They also offer an SDK[1] to make it easier to customize Voyage Linux.

## iMedia Embedded Linux

This is a hybrid between a small embedded Linux distribution and a mature distribution geared for X86 systems. While it

---

[1] http://linux.voyage.hk/develop

doesn't have the restrictions of an embedded distribution, it is more lightweight in terms of hard disk space, processor and memory requirements.

It is library-compatible with major distributions like Fedora Core, Gentoo, Suse or Mandriva and therefore makes it easy for the user to expand their installation. For computers based on AMD Geode LX and Geode GX processors there is *iMedia ALIX Linux*.

*iMedia Linux Appliances* are particularly interesting. These are pre-built Linux systems made for certain purposes like multimedia systems, kiosk systems, LAMP stacks, router appliances, MythTV and iMedia ALIX.

This distribution is normally installed via CD-ROM. One method is outlined in the iMedia Linux forums which explains how to use a USB CD-ROM to install iMedia Linux on ALIX machines that can't boot from a USB drive. I'll go into detail about this in the next chapter.

Personally I have not worked with *iMedia Linux* but I mention it here in case someone finds an appropriate appliance there.

## OpenWrt

OpenWrt is a Linux distribution for embedded devices. Instead of creating a single static firmware, OpenWrt delivers a fully writable system with software package management. This allows you to use software packages to customize the machine for any situation. OpenWrt is a system which allows developers to combine applications without having to create a complete firmware. For users it means being able to totallly adapt the machine in unforeseeable ways.

The Unified Configuration Interface (UCI) is particularly interesting. This offers a consistent configuration interface from the command line (the program *uci*) as well as in the web browser (*luci* with webserver).

Since the release of *Kamikaze*, OpenWrt has been usable on ALIX2 and ALIX3 as well as on WRAP machines from PC Engines.

The first boot takes a little longer, then the console is ready and can be activated by pressing <Enter>.

Once it is installed, all of the network devices found are combined in a network bridge that is accessible at the address 192.168.1.1. The computer can be configured via serial console, telnet or a webbrowser. After you have set a password for *root*, telnet access is disabled and SSH is enabled. To use the web interface with SSL, you'll need to install the package *luci-ssl*:

```
# opkg update
# opkg install luci-ssl
# /etc/init.d/uhttpd restart
```

## Read-only root with ext2 file system

There is one slight annoyance if you use OpenWrt with an ext2 file system. The file system is mounted read-write per default. This is one of the things I wanted to avoid. Luckily is an easy remedy: I insert the following line into the file */etc/rc.local* before exit 0 in the last line:

```
mount -o remount,ro /
```

Because I am lazy, I create two scripts named */sbin/remountrw* and */sbin/remountro* which contain the command above with the respective option to remount the file system read-write or read-only. To configure the system I have to unblock write access first:

```
# remountrw
# opkg update
# opkg install ...
# remountro
```

And the most important thing is to call up **remountro** at the end. That way the file system is mounted read-only and it doesn't matter if the power fails or the machine is switched off.

I can work well from the command line with these scripts. If I want to remount the file system read-write or read-only from the web interface *LuCI* I can use a small extension.

All extensions for *LuCI* go into the directories below */usr/lib/lua/luci/*. Control files go into the directory *controller/* while templates go under *view/*. The control file */usr/lib/lua/luci/controler/remount.lua* is short:

**remount.lua**

```lua
module("luci.controller.remount", package.seeall)
function index()
  local page = node("remount")
  page.sysauth = "root"
  page.sysauth_authenticator = "htmlauth"
  entry({"remount"}, template("remount"), "Remount")
  entry({"remount", "readonly"}, call("readonly"))
  entry({"remount", "readwrite"}, call("readwrite"))
end
function readwrite()
  luci.sys.exec("mount -o remount,rw,noatime /")
  luci.http.redirect(
    luci.dispatcher.build_url("remount")
  )
end
function readonly()
  luci.sys.exec("mount -o remount,ro /")
  luci.http.redirect(
    luci.dispatcher.build_url("remount")
  )
end
function mounted()
  local data = ""
  local partitions = luci.util.execi("mount")

  if not partitions then
    return "failure with mount command"
  end
```

```
29    for line in partitions do
30      if string.match(line,"^/.+%s/%s.+") then
31        data = data .. line .. "\n"
32      end
33    end
34    return data
35  end
```

This file registers a URL with the dispatcher in the function *index()*. Furthermore it provides the functions *readonly()*, *readwrite()* and *mounted()*. The first two remount the file system. The third extracts the line containing the root file system from the output of the *mount* command to show the current state.

**remount.htm**

```
1   <%+header%>
2   <h1><%:Remount%></h1>
3   <p> </p><br />
4   <% mounted = luci.controller.remount.mounted() %>
5   <pre>
6   <%=mounted%>
7   </pre>
8   <form name="readwrite" id="readwrite"
9       action="<%=controller%>/remount/readwrite"
10      target ="_self" style="display:inline">
11  <input type="submit" value="read-write" />
12  </form>
13  <form name="readonly" id="readonly"
14      action="<%=controller%>/remount/readonly"
```

```
15      target ="_self" style="display:inline">
16   <input type="submit" value="read-only" />
17   </form>
18   <%+footer%>
```

The template */usr/lib/lua/luci/view/remount.htm* is short too. It shows the return value of the function *mounted()*, mentioned above, and provides two buttons so you can select the functions *readwrite()* or *readonly()*.

Thus the extension to LuCI looks like this:

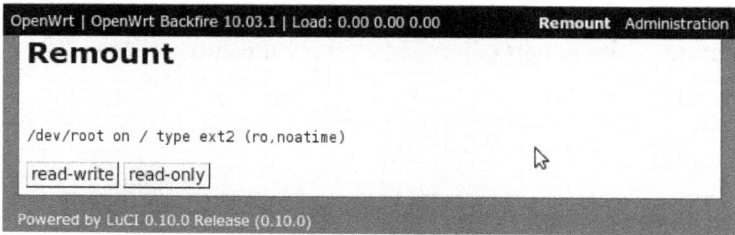

LuCI extension to remount the root partition

Here I must also remember to remount the root file system read-only when I'm done with configuring.

## Using the LEDs

To use the LEDs on OpenWrt I need the software package *kmods-leds-alix*. I can install this package in the command line with *opkg* or with LuCI. I can comfortably configure the LEDs using the web interface. Alternatively I can use *uci* in the command line. A sample configuration that lights LED1 constantly and shows the network traffic of eth0 at LED2 looks like this in the file */etc/config/system*:

```
1  config 'led'
2         option 'sysfs' 'alix:1'
3      option 'default' '1'
4      option 'trigger' 'default-on'
5
6  config 'led'
7      option 'default' '0'
8      option 'sysfs' 'alix:2'
9      option 'trigger' 'netdev'
10     option 'dev' 'eth0'
11     option 'mode' 'tx rx'
```

I can import this configuration in the command line like this:

```
# uci import system
```

## Slax

Slax is a Linux distribution specializing in small packed systems. It contains X windows, the KDE desktop with K-Office, a web browser, chat programs, audio, video and a number of other things. There are official editions in more than 20 languages.

Even though Slax is started from a compressed file system, all files are changeable, since the read-only file system is overlayed with a read-write AUFS file system.

This makes it a possible option for thin clients on ALIX machines with a graphics card.

## Linux From Scratch

The Linux From Scratch project is worth mentioning. It relays basic information about Linux in its own special way, which - together with tips from this book - can lead to a successful project on an ALIX machine.

## Buildroot

Buildroot is likewise not a Linux distribution but instead a project that assists the developer of a Linux system in choosing packages and configuring and building the root file system. It is designed for more experienced people who want or need to do and control things all be themselves.

It has a simple structure and basically relies on Makefile, which should be familiar to most developers. It can generate the necessary tools for cross compilation with *uClibc* or use available tools. The development and debugging tools can also be build for the target platform to make it easier to debug. Central components are *busybox* and *uClibc*. Buildroot supports various file system types for the root file system and more than a hundred software packages.

Homemade applications can be integrated into the system and are then built together with the rest of the system.

# Installing Linux

In this chapter I'll go into detail about different ways to install Linux for the first time on a machine.

Basically there are three ways:

1. I can prepare a CF boot medium on a second computer and insert this into the device.
2. I can boot and install from an USB stick. This only works for ALIX1.x as well as for ALIX.3D3 with AWARD BIOS. With the other models, in particular with TinyBIOS, I can't use USB as a boot medium.
3. I can boot and install using a network (PXE boot).

Of course it's also possible to combine these options.

## Preparing a boot medium on a second computer

This approach requires a computer with the ability to read and write CF cards. I now have various options.

The easiest and fastest way is to take a prebuilt image, which I can transfer to the CF card with the *dd* command (or something similar on a MS Windows machine). This method allows me to clone a machine or - in case of hardware failure - restore a machine really quickly. I might have to adapt some udev rules with regard to network adapters because these are bound to the hardware address on some distributions.

As an alternative to cloning an image with dd I can create the partitions and file systems manually, mount the file systems on the second computer and install the operating system using *debootstrap, tar, cpio* or something similar. Afterwards I have to install the boot loader on the CF card using *grub-install*.

Another possibility is to prepare the prospective system as a virtual machine (VM) and test everything including the serial console. When the system is ready I copy the VM "raw", that means bit for bit, onto the CF card. If I choose this option, I have to consider a few things:

- When creating the VM, it should be fully virtualized. Paravirtualization requires an environment that is not available on an ALIX board. In the best case I'll have installed too much software, in the worst case the system won't work at all.
- The hard disk of the VM shouldn't be larger than the CF card.
- Some hardware assignments, for instance the binding of an ethernet interface to a specific MAC address, may have to be opened in the *udev* rules.

I myself have not prepared a system in this way, but I consider it to be a viable approach if you want to alter a running system and there is no hardware available to test the changes thoroughly before deployment.

At the end, the CF card, which has been prepared in one of the different ways, is inserted into the ALIX machine and the device is ready to use.

## Preparing OpenWrt on another computer

OpenWrt allows me to easily prepare a CF card on another computer. There are different images on the download pages which I can write onto the CF card using *dd* and then insert into the machine. The *x86-generic* images with an ext2 file system are suitable for ALIX machines, for instance *openwrt-x86-generic-combined-ext2.img.gz*. This image contains a master boot record, a small partition with the boot loader *grub* and a partition with the root file system. After I have written the image onto the CF card, I can increase the size of the root partition using *gparted* or *parted*. Alternatively I can create another partition with another system on the CF card for experiments and add appropriate entries in the grub configuration of the first partition.

When preparing the CF card on another computer I have to open the case of the ALIX machine and then insert the card afterwards. Using the approaches below I can insert the CF card into the machine beforehand and directly install the system, using the ALIX machine itself.

# Installation using USB media

In the iMedia Linux forums I found the following procedure for installing the system from a USB CD-ROM onto an ALIX board with TinyBIOS:

1. Download a minimal CF archive from http://resources/imedialinux.com called *imedia-cfboot-x.y.zip*, where x.y stands for the version number.
2. Format a CF card with an ext2 file system.
3. Unpack the CF archive into the file system on the CF card.
4. Install the boot loader *GRUB* on the CF card.
5. Burn the installation CD-ROM and connect a USB CD-ROM drive to the ALIX board.
6. Insert the CF card into the ALIX board and start it. The mini-operating system on the CF cards starts, mounts the CD-ROM and installs from the CD-ROM.

On ALIX.1 you an alternatively try to create a USB live system with *UNetbootin* and start the machine with it. I haven't yet tested this sort of ALIX.1 board.

## Installation using PXE-Boot

In my opinion the most elegant and flexible solution is to install the system with PXE boot via a network.

Here the computer loads the boot loader from the network. The boot loader loads the programs needed for the installation and these install the operating system. This way I can work with a completely assembled machine and don't have to open the case before or after installation. I only have to take care that the machine starts in PXE-boot mode.

> **Tip**
>
> On a PC Engines ALIX I have to press n on the serial console while it is testing the memory in order to boot in PXE-boot mode once.
>
> If I press s instead, I enter setup mode. There I can press e to set PXE as permanent boot mode. Afterwards I exit setup by pressing q and confirm my changes. I can unset the PXE boot the same way.

One PXE-boot installation is not like the other. There are various ways to individualize them or automate them.

## Standard Debian installation using PXE-boot

Here the boot loader starts a mini system containing the Debian installer.

I first prepare a DHCP server for a PXE-boot by using ISC DHCPd. I can do this for one host depending on the number of devices, I want to install:

```
host hostname {
  next-server bootservername;
  filename "bootladerfile";
  hardware ethernet 01:02:03:04:05:06;
}
```

Or I can do it for a group of similar devices:

```
 1  group {
 2    next-server bootservername;
 3    filename "bootladerdatei";
 4    host hostname1 {
 5        hardware ethernet 01:02:03:04:05:06;
 6    }
 7    host hostname2 {
 8        hardware ethernet 01:02:03:04:05:07;
 9    }
10  }
```

The entry *bootservername* refers to the TFTP server for the boot loader. This TFTP server should understand the option *tsize*, for instance *tftp-hpa*. I use **pxelinux.0** from *PXELINUX* as a *bootloader file* which is part of the *SYSLINUX* project. I put the files of the Debian installer in a directory tree under the TFTP root file system. The configuration for *PXELINUX* is in a file in the directory *pxelinux.cfg* under the TFTP root and looks like this for the Debian installer:

```
1  SERIAL 0 38400 0
2  DEFAULT install
3  LABEL install
4    kernel d-i/i386/linux
5    append initrd=d-i/i386/initrd.gz -- \
6           console=ttyS0,38400n80
```

In this example I stored the files of the Debian installer in the directory *d-i/i386*. (The line break before console= is just for the formatting of this book. This line belongs to the append line.)

This installation is interactive just like a normal installation from a CD-ROM. I have the same options within the constraints of the hardware. Because the installation is interactive, it also ties up my time. There is little else I can do in the meantime except use *Preseed* to respond to the questions of the Debian installer in the debconf database.

## Installation using PXE-Initrd

In my opinion, using *pxe-initrd* is a little better. This is a collection of scripts and configuration files which allow you to boot a Linux system using PXE, format the hard disks and copy the operating system afterwards from a server using *rsync*. Everything works fully automatically without the need for interaction.

> **Tip**
>
> I have different files for *localboot* and *pxe-initrd* on the TFTP server in the directory *pxelinux.cf*.
>
> The file named *default*, which is used for all systems that don't otherwise fit has this content:
>
> ```
> 1  default localboot
> 2
> 3    label localboot
> 4    localboot 0
> ```
>
> This configuration means the machine boots the locally installed system, in case the computer accidentally boots with PXE enabled.

For all systems where *Voyage Linux 0.7.5* is to be installed the file *voyage-0.7.5.conf* contains the following:

```
1  serial 0 38400
2  console 0
3  label linux
4      KERNEL vmlinuz-2.6.38-voyage
5      APPEND initrd=initrd-2.6.38-voyage \
6             console=ttyS0,38400n1 \
7             root=/dev/hda1 root_size=768
```

It uses this to load the kernel and the initramfs for the *Voyage Linux* version. (The line break before console= and root= is just for the formatting of this book. Both lines belong to the APPEND line.).

In a posting from 2009 on the mailing list *[voyage-linux]* I found a note on *jra-initrd* from Jeff R. Allen. Back then he had taken *bit-pxe* and modified it to fit his needs. When I tested his scripts with Voyage Linux version 0.7.5 I found that his scripts no longer worked. I adapted the scripts from *jra-initrd* in October 2011, customized them to fit my needs and published them as *pxe-initrd* (please see the appendix for sources). These scripts do work with version 0.8, but they still have to be tested with newer versions.

The operating system you want to install is stored as a directory tree on a server and made available through an *rsync* server. The scripts on the initramfs format the local CF card, mount the file systems and copy the operating system using *rsync*. Afterwards the boot loader *grub* is installed and the machine reboots. No interaction is necessary to do all this and everything is determined beforehand. All I have to do is to make sure that the operating system doesn't get installed again after rebooting. Either I only start the ALIX machine once with a PXE boot by pressing n during the memory test or I change the PXELINUX configuration on the TFTP server to `localboot` after installation has begun.

Pxe-initrd has the advantage of being quick to setup and I don't need a complex infrastructure. Instead, in the simplest case I need *pxe-initrd*, a directory tree with the operating system I want to install, *dnsmasq* and *rsync* as well as a free ethernet interface if I don't want to install the new machines in the production network. The installation itself needs absolutely no interaction. Once it is started I'm able to do something else and come back later. To a certain extent I can control the installation retrospectively, that means at boot time with kernel parameters. And I can modify the directory tree containing the operating system by doing a `chroot` in the root directory and modifying it from within.

This has some disadvantages. For instance the modification is a little bit cumbersome since I have to do a `chroot` in the root directory, where I do not have the whole environment like a normal system (*procfs*, *sysfs* and device files are lacking in the chroot environment). For most changes I do not need these, for others there are workarounds (such as additionally mounting these file systems in the chroot environment). Some software packages can only be installed using a few tricks. Furthermore I need complete directory trees for all of the systems I want to install and therefore more hard disk space.

> **Tip**
>
> The *postinit* script of the *busybox-syslogd* package tries to start the demon program which fails in the chroot environment. Thus installation is incomplete, something which I can't repair easily with `apt-get -f install`. In this case the following trick will help:
>
> ```
> # chmod -x /etc/init.d/busybox-syslogd
> # chmod -x /etc/init.d/busybox-klogd
> # apt-get -f install
> # chmod +x /etc/init.d/busybox-syslogd
> # chmod +x /etc/init.d/busybox-klogd
> ```
>
> If I modify both scripts to prevent the demon programs from starting, the *postinit* script doesn't start these programs which ensures an error-free installation.

## PXE installation with FAI

FAI (Fully Automated Installation) is the fine art of automatic installation of Debian based Linux. This installation system is well-engineered and therefore needs quite a bit of time to comprehend, especially if you want to exploit all its possibilities. But it is worth the time if you have several different systems and regularly want or have to setup new systems.

Together with other tools for automating system administration tasks, like *cfengine*, *puppet* or *chef* it makes the daily routine of the system administrator tremendously easier, but I digress.

FAI's main advantage over pxe-initrd is its extreme flexibility. Completely interaction free installation is possible because the installed systems at the end of a successful installation automatically change their configuration at the TFTP server to *localboot*.

The systems you want to install aren't adapted individually. Instead you define classes that match the systems requirements and the system gets installed according to the defined classes. Everything can be planned beforehand and FAI installs the system according to the plan.

There are a few disadvantages, which your project should take into consideration. You will need the right infrastructure, including a DHCP server, a TFTP server and an additional NFS server. These three are often combined in the so-called FAI server. The time you'll need to become familiar with FAI adds to the project time. Everything has to be planned beforehand. FAI only installs the plan.

All in all, in my opinion FAI is nevertheless the silver bullet. If you are already using it or intend to use it anyway for other machines, just give it a try.

In the end, everyone has to decide for themselves how to get their Linux system onto the ALIX machine in order to move on to the next steps of their project.

# Components of a Linux system

In this chapter I will go into detail about the components that make up a Linux system. To do this, I divided the system into the following areas:

**Kernel**
> The glue that holds everything together.

**File system**
> The place where everything (programs and data) is permanently deposited.

**RAM**
> All of the programs and data must be copied here before they can be used. Most of the time little consideration is given to this topic. Because these machines only have a little RAM, I believe a few thoughts are appropriate.

**I/O system**
> This provides the basis for communicating with the environment via the network, serial connections, keyboard, screen and other means.

**System programs**
> All of the programs which aren't vital for the intended use of the machine, but are instead there to maintain stable operation.

**User programs**
All programs which are vital for the intended use of the machine.

Of course these areas overlap and some programs may be considered to be a system program or a user program - depending on what they are being used for.

# Kernel

The kernel is - rightly so - only considered a component of the total system. Efforts are being made, for instance with Debian, to make the operating system usable with the BSD kernel or with Hurd. Nevertheless the kernel plays a central role in the overall system as the gateway between hardware and software, as communication interface between the various processes running and as the entity that allocates the resources to the processes.

Of particular interest is the amount of support the kernel gives to the hardware in the ALIX machines and whether I need external kernel modules or whether I can get by with Userland programs.

> **Tip**
>
> *The Geode LX800 processor is not compatible with i686.*
>
> Since there are no more i586 software packages from Debian, I have to install the i486 versions.

## Kernel modules

The standard kernel includes GPL drivers for all of the hardware plugged into the ALIX boards.

**leds-alix**
: This modul is used to control the LEDs on the boards. The ledtrig-* modules provide activation triggers. Since kernel version 2.6.30, these modules have been included in the standard kernel. That means I don't need separate modules for Debian 6 Squeeze. For older kernels (for instance from Debian 5 Lenny), I need the package *leds-alix-source* which I can compile and install with *module-assistant* (m-a).

**rtc** I need this module to access the hardware clock.

**geode-aes, geode-rng**
: The AMD Geode LX800 processor, which is built into some of the ALIX boards, contains an on-chip AES 128-bit crypto accelerations block and a true random number generator. It is faster to use these than the algorithms used in the software and frees up the CPU for other purposes. I need rngd from the *rng-tools* to use the hardware random number generator.

**geodewdt**
: A watchdog driver is available starting in kernel version 2.6.33 which restarts the computer automatically if it gets stuck.

**i2c_core**
: This module for the I²C bus is needed to access the sensors

**lm90**
> This is the driver for the sensor chip. Currently it identifies a lm86 sensor.

**scx200_acb**
> This is the driver for the ACCESS bus of the Geode processors and the CS5536 chips.

**cs5535_gpio**
> The GPIO module to access the LEDs and button comes with kernel version 2.6.33 and above, otherwise it must be compiled as an additional kernel module.

**cs5536, pata_cs5536**
> Modules for the compact flash "hard disk". Depending on the kernel version and kernel options, the CF card is accessible either as */dev/hda* or */dev/sda*. This can lead to problems at boot time if you want to test another kernel version. In this case it would be better to identify the disk using its UUID or label.

| cs5536 | ATA Stack -> /dev/sda |
|---|---|
| pata_cs5536 | PATA Stack -> /dev/hda |

**via_rhine**
> The ethernet module.

# File system

The file system is the place where everything that amounts to the system (programs, data) is stored permanently. It pays to look a little bit closer at this. On the one hand the various file systems are to a greater or lesser extent suitable for the different media. Particularly with regard to flash media I want to avoid writing on the same spot over and over and to use at least the operating system data in read-only to minimize damages caused by excessive write access. On the other hand some programs need permanent storage to save data after a reboot or if there is not enough RAM available.

If I have mounted the root file system read-only there are still ways to enable write access for processes:

- With overlay file systems like AUFS
- By mounting writable file systems like *tmpfs* at certain mount points
- With symbolic links to writable file systems

## SquashFS

This is a compressed read-only file system for Linux from version 2.4 and above. The kernel accesses this file system through a kernel modul as virtual file system (VFS). SquashFS has been included in the standard kernel since kernel version 2.6.29. For lower kernel versions a separate module has to be compiled.

The entire UID and GID as well the file creation time are stored in SquashFS. Duplicate files are stored only once. Files are compressed with deflate (zlib) or with the more effective Lempel-Zif-Markow algorithm (LZMA). SquashFS is often used together with *UnionFS* or the more modern *AUFS* to allow the processes at least temporary write access.

To work with SquashFS on Debian you have to install the package *squashfs-tools* which contains the programs *mksquash* for creating it and *unsquashfs* for extracting a SquashFS without mounting it. MS Windows at least offers read access with *7-zip*.

For initial experiments you can convert a part of your file system into a SquashFS:

```
# mksquashfs /usr/local /mnt/local.sqsh
...
# du -s /mnt/local.sqsh /usr/local
94156    /mntlocal.sqsh
219252   /usr/local/
```

The newly formed SquashFS is already considerably smaller than the original file system. Since I want to try out the SquashFS together with the overlay file system AUFS, I create three mount points:

```
# mkdir /mnt/local
# mkdir /mnt/local-ro
# mkdir /mnt/local-rw
# mount /mnt/local.sqsh /mnt/local-ro -t squashfs \
  -o loop
# mount -t aufs \
  -o dirs=/mnt/local-rw=rw:/mnt/local-ro=ro \
  aufs /mnt/local
# mount
...
/dev/loop0 on /mnt/local-ro type squashfs (rw)
aufs on /mnt/local type aufs \
(rw,dirs=/mnt/local-rw=rw:/mnt/local-ro=ro)
```

The SquashFS is mounted at /mnt/local-ro/ where it is read-only. I want to use this file system read-write at /mnt/local/. AUFS redirects all my write access to /mnt/local-rw/:

```
# echo foo> /mnt/local-ro/var/foo
-bash: /mnt/local-ro/var/foo: file system is read-only
# echo foo> /mnt/local/var/foo
# diff -r /mnt/local-ro /usr/local
# diff -r /mnt/local /usr/local
Nur in /mnt/local/var: foo.
# cat /mnt/local/var/foo
foo
# cat /mnt/local-rw/var/foo
foo
```

I can't write to /mnt/local-ro/, even though *mount* showed that it was mounted read-write, since this is impossible with SquashFS. Therefore I create the file in /mnt/local/ and find it eventually in /mnt/local-rw/.

## Overlay root file system with AUFS

With this solution the root file system gets mounted read-only and there is an AUFS laid over the whole directory tree which redirects all write access to a temporary file system in RAM (tmpfs). The whole thing is set up through a script in the InitRD which moves the root partiton to /ro/, mounts a *tmpfs* at /rw/ and an AUFS at /, reads from /ro/ and writes to /rw/. This script is activated by the kernel command line argument *aufs=tmpfs*. Furthermore, the script creates two other scripts named *remountrw* and *remountro*, which can remount the root partition at */ro/* in read-write mode or read-only mode. I set up my first ALIX systems this way.

Everything that gets written by any program into any file ends up in tmpfs, as long as there is enough RAM available and disappears after a reboot. If I want to make some changes permanent, I have to call up *remountrw*, move the changes from */rw/* to */ro/* and then call up *remountro*.

One advantage of this solution is that I don't have to think about which program is trying to write which file. Everything goes into tmpfs and is gone after rebooting.

The downside is that system upgrades also land under */rw/* and have to be copied afterwards to */ro/*. Alternatively I can start the system without the kernel option *aufs=tmpfs* and boot the system just like any normal system. This is not a very good option for systems which are supposed to run permanently. Therefore I turn to the next solution which is used, among others, by *Voyage Linux*.

## Read-only root file system with multiple tmpfs

The central idea of this solution is to mount the root file system read-only and to not allow any process to write to this file system. For directories that traditionally contain writable files (e.g. */var/run/*) I mount *tmpfs* (RAM disks) at these points to allow write access.

For the directories */var/run/* and */var/lock/* this is already available in standard Debian Linux if I set the following in the file */etc/default/rcS*:

```
1  # /etc/default/rcS
2  # ...
3  RAMRUN=yes
4  RAMLOCK=yes
```

This is even better supported in Voyage Linux. Here I can specify further directories to be mounted as tmpfs in the file */etc/default/voyate-util* by adding them to the variable *VOYAGE_SYNC_DIRS*. These directories are also automatically saved at shutdown, and filled with the saved files at system boot. If I want to manually save the files in these directories, I do it like this:

```
# remountrw
# /etc/init.d/voyage-sync sync
# remountro
```

With this solution I have to think about which directories should be writable (for instance the directory with the leases of the DHCP demon). But afterwards a system upgrade is as easy as this:

```
# remountrw
# apt-get update && apt-get upgrade
# /etc/init.d/voyage-sync sync
# remountro
```

This is why I moved away from the AUFS solution and am now using Voyage Linux on my ALIX machines.

The package *flashybrid* on standard Debian GNU/Linux functions similarly to *voyage-util* on Voyage Linux.

> **Tip**
>
> The package *flashybrid* from Debian isn't as low maintenance as *voyage-util* from Voyage Linux. With a few adjustments, however, it does do what I want it to do.
>
> 1. After installating the package I set the variable `ENABLED=yes` in the file */etc/default/flashybrid*.
> 2. I create a directory */ram/* under which *flashybrid* mounts all the *tmpfs*.
> 3. I configure the maximum RAM for the *tmpfs* in the file */etc/flashybrid/config*.
> 4. I determine which directories are to be provided as RAM-disk in the file */etc/flashybrid/ramstore*. These are filled from the root partition at boot time and saved at shutdown with *fh-sync*.
> 5. I configure all of the directories which only contain temporary files in */etc/flashybrid/ramtmp*.
> 6. To make sure that */etc/init.d/flashybrid* gets started at boot time, I use `insserv flashybrid`.
> 7. Some servics are started before *flashybrid* and keep files in the root file system open. To close these files, I have to use this workaround in */etc/rc.local*:
>
> ```
> /etc/init.d/rsyslog restart
> /etc/init.d/cron restart
> /etc/init.d/nfs-common restart
> /etc/init.d/portmap restart
> mountro
> ```
>
> To find out which services have to be restarted, please see chapter Strategies for problem solving.

Flashybrid provides the commands *mountro*, *mountrw* and *fh-sync*, which have the same function as their corresponding commands in Voyage Linux.

## Writable file systems

If I need a writable file system for my project, I recommend a modern CF card (with CompactFlash 5.0 or later) that supports the TRIM command. Together with a suitable file system (*btrfs*, *ext4fs*, *fat* or *gfs2*) and a current kernel (starting with version 2.6.33) the operating system can tell the CF card which sectors aren't needed anymore and no longer need to be copied. By doing this, and by leaving some space free, I can extend the lifetime of the CF card.

## Identifying partitions with UUID or label

Depending on the kernel version and options, the first CF card will either be called */dev/hda* or */dev/sda*. Thus the system boot may fail if I just want to test a new kernel. In this case it may be beneficial to identify the partition using its UUID. To do this, I do the following:

After the machine has booted I look in */dev/disk/by-uuid/* to find out the UUID of the individual partitions have:

```
$ ls -l /dev/disk/by-uuid/
total 0
lrwxrwxrwx 1 root root 10 2011-11-25 07:43
f779141e-e3b1-4521-9333-9dde9de0b64f -> ../../sda1
```

(Output is wrapped for better legibility.)

Afterwards I change the entry for */dev/sda1* in the file */etc/fstab* to `UUID=f779141e-e3b1-4521-9333-9dde9de0b64f` and do the same for the other partitions. I change the kernel option *root* in the Grub boot entry (file */boot/grub/menu.lst*) accordingly:

```
root=/dev/disk/by-uuid/f779141e-...-9dde9de0b64f
```

Another possibility is to use filesystem labels. I can use *e2label*, for instance, to write these on an *ext2fs*.

```
# e2label /dev/sda1 rootfs
```

I change the line for the root file system in */etc/fstab* like this:

```
LABEL=rootfs    /    ext3    errors=remount-ro 0 1
```

And the Grub boot entry looks like this for the kernel option *root*:

```
root=LABEL=rootfs
```

## Random Access Memory

Before programs and data can be used by the CPU, they have to be copied into RAM. This is where everything happens, but this type of memory is also often scarce on these small computers. This is the most important thing that can be said about RAM, but because I consider RAM to be so important, I want to go further into detail.

In order to execute a programm in a process, it has to be loaded into RAM. Only the parts of the program that will be executed next get loaded and not the whole program (except when the whole program fits onto a single page, but you'll have a hard time finding such a program). If a program is used by different processes it will only be loaded once. Only the stack and the heap are used privately by the process. It is advisable to look out for programs, which don't use much memory but still provide the functionality you need. It is also advantageous whan a program like *busybox* can replace as many other programs as possible because you save memory in RAM and on the file system when it can be used by many processes.

I will need more RAM if I use RAM directly as a file system through overlay file systems, tmpfs or loopback mounts. This RAM is no longer available as working memory for processes.

Finally the kernel uses all of the memory that is not used for any of the purposes mentioned above as a buffer for file system access. I usually don't need to pay attention to this because this memory is automatically freed up when it is needed for other purposes.

The main memory of the X86 computer architecture is divided into three areas:

**ZONE_DMA**
> from 0 to 16 MiB. This range contains memory pages which may be used by devices for DMA.

**ZONE_NORMAL**
> from 16 MiB to 896 MiB. This range contains regular memory pages.

**ZONE_HIGHMEM**
> over 896 MiB. This range contains memory pages, which are not continuously available in the address space of the 32-bit CPU. This range has no relevance for ALIX computers.

## Analyzing memory usage

I can use the programs *free*, *top*, *ps* and *pmap* in order to analyze the memory usage of a Linux system.

The program **free** gives me an overview of the current allocation of the total usable system memory:

```
$ free
                 total      used      free shared buffers  cached
Mem:            255488    135984    119504      0    6588  108732
-/+ buffers/cache:        20664    234824
Swap:                0         0         0
```

I am never able to see the entire memory under *total* because the memory used by the hardware and the kernel has been calculated out.

The memory labelled *buffers* contains temporary data from the processes running, like input queues, file buffers, output queues and so on. The memory marked *cached* contains buffered file accesses, for instance if multiple processes are accessing the same file.

I can use the program *top* to isolate processes which use a particularly large amount of memory. It provides an overview of the processes, CPU load and total memory consumption in the head lines and below these there is a table containing the data of the individual processes. The output is updated continuously and can be modified. By pressing ? I am able to call up a brief help page explaining the possible modifications. It is interesting to sort the table by memory consumption, which I can do by pressing m:

Output mangled to fit

```
top - 08:29:03 up 125 days, 21:33,  1 user,  load a..
Tasks:  54 total,   1 running,  53 sleeping,   0 st..
Cpu(s):  0.4%us,  0.2%sy,  0.0%ni, 99.4%id,  0.0%wa..
Mem:     255488k total,   136172k used,    119316k fr..
Swap:        0k total,        0k used,        0k fr..

  PID USER    ..VIRT  RES  SHR..%MEM    TIME+  COMMAND
 9006 mathias..6220 4924 1340.. 1.9   0:03.21 bash
 1031 snmp   ..8832 4268 2660.. 1.7 186:43.97 snmpd
  954 ntp    ..4576 1920 1480.. 0.8   9:52.96 ntpd
 9037 mathias..2324 1096  876.. 0.4   0:00.74 top
 9005 root   ..2396 1048  788.. 0.4   0:01.44 dropbear
  898 root   ..3808  928  740.. 0.4   0:27.43 cron
 2260 root   ..2960  900  672.. 0.4   0:06.71 pppd
  842 dnsmasq..4116  840  656.. 0.3   0:14.54 dnsmasq
  220 root   ..2252  720  396.. 0.3   0:00.23 udevd
```

```
263 root     ..2248  688   364.. 0.3    0:00.06 udevd
```

The following columns are the most important columns for analyzing memory:

**VIRT**
: stands for the virtual size of the process. This includes all code, data and shared libraries plus pages that have been swapped out and pages that have been mapped but not used. In other words all of the memory this process could use.

**RES** is the resident size. This is the physical memory of a process which has not been swapped out to disk. This is used to compute the value of the *%MEM* column.

**SHR** is the shared memory size. This is the part of *VIRT* that can be shared with other processes.

**%MEM**
: the percentage of the available physical memory which the process currently uses. I use this column (and sort this column by pressing m) to find the processes and programs which use the most memory and are therefore candidates for further investigation.

Using the program *ps* I can get a snapshot of the memory currently being consumed by all of the processes:

Output mangled to fit

```
$ ps aux
USER       PID %CPU %MEM  VSZ  RSS TTY..COMMAND
root         1  0.0  0.2 2024  676 ?  ..init [2]
root         2  0.0  0.0    0    0 ?  ..[kthreadd]
root         3  0.0  0.0    0    0 ?  ..[ksoftirqd/0]
root         4  0.0  0.0    0    0 ?  ..[watchdog/0]
root         5  0.0  0.0    0    0 ?  ..[events/0]
...
snmp      1031  0.1  1.6 8832 4268 ?  ../usr/sbin/snmpd
root      1033  0.0  0.1 1480  396 ?  ../usr/sbin/udhcp
root      1056  0.0  0.2 1700  536 tty../sbin/getty -L
root      1305  0.0  0.2 2248  544 ?  ..udevd --daemon
root      2260  0.0  0.3 2960  900 ?  ../usr/sbin/pppd
root      9005  0.0  0.4 2396 1048 ?  ../usr/sbin/dropb
mathias   9006  0.1  1.9 6220 4928 pts..-bash
root      9041  0.0  0.0    0    0 ?  ..[flush-8:0]
mathias   9042  0.0  0.3 2344  904 pts..ps aux
```

To find out which process is consuming the most memory I sort by column 6:

**Output mangled to fit**

```
$ ps aux|sort -n -k6 -r |head
mathias 9006   0.1  1.9 6220 4928 pts...-bash
snmp    1031   0.1  1.6 8832 4268 ?    ../usr/sbin/snmpd
ntp      954   0.0  0.7 4576 1920 ?    ../usr/sbin/ntpd
root    9005   0.0  0.4 2396 1048 ?    ../usr/sbin/dropb
root     898   0.0  0.3 3808  928 ?    ../usr/sbin/cron
mathias 9054   0.0  0.3 2344  908 pts..ps aux
root    2260   0.0  0.3 2960  900 ?    ../usr/sbin/pppd
dnsmasq  842   0.0  0.3 4116  840 ?    ../usr/sbin/dnsma
mathias 9057   0.0  0.3 2036  768 pts..less -S
root     220   0.0  0.2 2252  720 ?    ..udevd --daemon
```

The columns *VSZ* (virtual set size, 5), *RSS* (resident set size, 6) and *PID* (process id, 2) are the most interesting for analyzing memory. I use the last one to investigate a process further using *pmap*:

**Output mangled to fit**

```
$ sudo pmap -d 1031
1031:   /usr/sbin/snmpd -Lsd -Lf /dev/null -u snmp \
-g snmp -I -smux -p /var/run/snmpd.pid
Address   Kbytes Mode  Offset    Device    Mapping
08048000      24 r-x-- 0..00000  000:00010 snmpd
0804e000       4 rw--- 0..05000  000:00010 snmpd
09cd4000    1156 rw--- 0..00000  000:00000 [ anon ]
b70bf000      40 r-x-- 0..00000  000:00010 libnss_fi...
```

```
b70c9000       4 r---- 0..09000 000:00010 libnss_fi...
b70ca000       4 rw--- 0..0a000 000:00010 libnss_fi...
...
b77c7000       4 r-x-- 0..00000 000:00000    [ anon ]
b77c8000     108 r-x-- 0..00000 000:00010 ld-2.11.2.so
b77e3000       4 r---- 0..1a000 000:00010 ld-2.11.2.so
b77e4000       4 rw--- 0..1b000 000:00010 ld-2.11.2.so
bfc54000     332 rw--- 0..00000 000:00000   [ stack ]
mapped: 8828K   writeable/private: 2172K   shared: 0K
```

The memory marked *writable/private* in the last line of the output is the memory that the process uses only for itself and doesn't share with other processes.

## Swappiness

If I have to swap memory, despite all of my efforts to reduce memory consumption, I can at least influence whether the kernel prefers to swap out processes and data or reduce buffer caches when all of the free memory is taken. I have to use a kernel version of at least 2.6 to do this. There is a parameter *swappiness* which is adjusted as an integer between 0 and 100. 100 means the kernel prefers to swap out processes and 0 means the kernel first reduces buffer caches. The default is 60; a value of 20 or less is recommended for laptops. You can change this value at runtime like this:

```
# sysctl -w vm.swappiness = 30
```

or:

```
# echo 30 > /proc/sys/vm/swappiness
```

If the system runs without swap memory, this parameter is irrelevant.

## I/O subsystem

The I/O subsystem's job is to communicate with the environment. The kernel is responsible for allocating the devices and the low level drivers. Here I find the drivers suitable to do this.

It is very important to first identify the hardware built into the computer. There are a few programs which I can use to do this:

*lspci*
> lists the devices on the PCI bus.

*lsusb*
> does the same for the USB.

*lscpu*
> provides information about the CPU which supplements the information from */proc/cpuinfo*

*lshw*
> finds out nearly everything about the hardware that can be found using software.

*dmesg*
> shows the kernel messages and, particularly with false identified hardware, can show the kernel's view or show whether it has recognized this hardware at all.

Using the output of these programs in an internet search, I can usually find the right driver for hardware hitherto unknown to me.

## System programs

These are programs that are not concerned with the overall purpose of the system but rather to ensure the operational availability.

The first process to load after the system boots is *init*. Traditionally there are *System-V* and *BSD* init programs that work in a similar fashion and only differ in the way they process the start and stop scripts of the systems services. Because most traditional services were geared towards server systems that would boot very infrequently, the *init* programs can not be optimized easily for a fast system boot. Therefore recent projects have been trying to find a substitute for *init* that allows more flexibility and shorter boot times for the entire system.

Other important system programs for logging into the system are *getty* for the serial console on ALIX and *sshd* which enables you to login via the network. These programs are actually designed for the system's user but I regard the system administrator to be a user who has to log in to acquire an overview of the system or to diagnose a problem. In the same way the display manager on a graphical system or an HTTP server with a web administration system could be regarded as a system program.

> **Tip**
>
> I like using *dropbear* as an SSH demon. It is designed for environments with little memory. It implements most of the features of the SSH2 protocol and others like X11 and authentication agent forwarding.

I consider *syslogd* and *klogd* to be essential for every system. These often provide valuable hints should errors arise and, if monitored regularly, help to avoid some problems beforehand. I need a *syslogd* that uses resources sparingly, especially on limited platforms like ALIX machines. I have had good experiences with *busybox-syslogd*. It doesn't write to files but uses a memory range of a certain size for the log messages and can forward them to external log servers. I can use *logread* to read the local messages.

Because many systems which use the network to work together, depend on synchronous clocks (to correlate log messages, for cryptographic systems like *kerberos* and other things), I consider *ntp* to be essential as well. In a system without a network this may not be required.

I use an SNMP demon if I want to use this protocol to monitor the device.

> **Tip**
>
> In Debian's default settings, *snmpd* logs every access. This

is particularly annoying if, for instance with Nagios, access occurs at short intervals. Then I have a system log with data which is not relevant to the problem. To prevent this I have to change the command line parameter for logging. The original option for logging using *syslogd* is -Lsd. In my opinion -LSwd is better which means only messages with a priority of *warning* or above are logged to *syslogd*. This has to be changed in the file */etc/default/snmp* in the variable *SNMPDOPTS* and afterwards I have to restart *snmpd*.

## User programs

These depend on the purpose of the machine. They can be DHCP, DNS, HTTP or other servers, MP3 streaming clients, or Asterisk for a telephone system.

Due to the wide range of possible application fields and the array of available programs, I won't go into detail here.

# Compiling software yourself

I don't always find all software I need in the repositories of my chosen Linux distribution. Sometimes I am lucky and find packages for my distribution on the software's homepage which I can use immediately. Other times it helps to look in the developer areas of my distribution. Debian, for example, offers the *Stable* branch, which I normally use for such projects, as well as a branch called *Testing* and another called *Unstable*, which may contain the software I am looking for. I often can't directly use this because programs from the other branches need other libraries not found in the *Stable* branch. Sometimes it's sufficient to rebuild these packages on a machine running the *Stable* branch. Often I need library packages that I have to rebuild as well. For some software packages this has already been done. These can be found at http://backports.debian.org. The advantage here is that I can use the package management from Debian by simply including a few lines in */etc/apt/sources.list*.

## System or user software

If I want to install software for which there is no support at all in my distribution, I have to manage this software myself. This means that I have to compile, install, and configure it myself.

And if I replace it with a newer version, I have to deinstall the old version.

Often there are files called README or INSTALL in the source archives which contain hints on compilation, required libraries and installation. I have a look here first.

Many software packages use the GNU Build System, also known as *Autotools*, which facilitates porting to different UNIX environments and checks the requirements for building it on my computer. These are recognizable by their executable file *configure* in the root of the software package. I can call up `./configure --help` to get hints about further options. These allow me to switch certain features on or off, or preset some paths for later installation. In most cases I am interested in the option `--prefix` which determines where the software is installed when I call up `make install` at the end.

Usually this is preset to */usr/local* so that the software doesn't collide with the distributions package management under that directory. I prefer the directory */usr/local/stow/softwarename-version*. This enables me to use the program stow to create symbolic links to the directory under */usr/local* so that I can use it with the conventional paths. If I install another version later, this is installed in a totally different directory so that I can switch between these versions within seconds. This also makes removing an older version easier because I only have to remove everything under that corresponding directory. This facilitates the management of self-compiled software tremendously.

As an example the installation of *monotone* a distributed revision control system, looks like this on my computers:

```
$ tar xjf monotone-1.0.tar.bz2
$ cd monotone-1.0
$ ./configure --prefix=/usr/local/stow/monotone-1.0
$ make
$ make check
$ sudo make install
$ sudo stow -d /usr/local/stow monotone-1.0
```

Afterwards I have monotone installed under */usr/local/stow/monotone-1.0* and there are symbolic links under */usr/local/bin*, */usr/local/etc* and */usr/local/share* which refer to the files under the previously mentioned directory. I can call up mtn directly, the manual page is available using man mtn and if I ever want to get rid of it, all I have to do is to call up *stow* with option -D (and remove everything under */usr/local/stow/monotone-1.0* if I need the storage).

## Creating Debian Packages

There are at least three reasons why I would need to create a Debian software package myself:

- The software I want exists as a Debian package but I need a version or feature which is not contained in the distribution.
- I actually don't want the software but other software packages depend on it so that the package manager always tries to install this software.
- I want to deploy the software using the Debian package management.

In the first case I can make it easy on myself. I obtain the latest source packages with `apt-get source packagename`. Then I retrieve the version of the pristine software that I need. Now I can copy the *debian* directory of the source package to the extracted pristine source directory. I take a look at the files under *debian* and possibly adapt them if necessary to unlock certain features. Afterwards I call up `debuild -us -uc` in the root directory of the source. With a little luck I obtain the software in the form I need it in.

In the second case I want to have an empty package which complies with the dependencies and manage the software myself under */usr/local* as described in the previous section. I can use the tool *equivs* for this which was designed especially for this purpose.

In the third case I have to learn how to build Debian software packages. First I install the essential software for developing packages:

**build-essential**
> This meta package contains a list of packages necessary to develop Debian packages.

**devscripts**
> This contains scripts to make the life of a Debian package developer easier.

**debhelper**
> This is a collection of programs which can be used in the *debian/rules* file to automate common tasks in package building.

*puilder* or *sbuild*
> With this software you can build your packages in a chroot environment to avoid certain security problems with unchecked software and to recognise dependencies more easily.

For beginners I recommend the article *HowToPackageForDebian* in the Debian Wiki (wiki.debian.org).

## Kernel and kernel modules

For Debian based systems I can refer to the *Debian Linux Kernel Handbook* for questions regarding the kernel.

Chapter four, *Common kernel related tasks* provides help in most cases. In order to compile the kernel or some extra modules myself, I need some developer packages which I can install with *apt-get*:

*build-essential*
> Was already mentioned above.

*kernel-package*
> This contains resources for Debian packages covering the Linux kernel. Among other things it contains *make-kpkg*, which helps build a kernel package that can be installed with dpkg.

*module-assistant*
> This helps compile external kernel modules which are already prepared for Debian (like for instance *openafs-modules-source*).

## Compiling the kernel

First I install the necessary developer packages:

```
$ sudo apt-get install build-essential
$ sudo apt-get install kernel-package
```

Next I obtain the kernel sources. I either use a suitable Debian package *linux-source-$version* or I take the sources from www.kernel.org[2] and extract them under */usr/src*.

Afterwards I create a symbolic link from */usr/src/linux* to the extracted kernel source directory and configure the kernel. For this I can take the configuration of a running kernel as a starting point:

```
$ sudo ln -s linux-<version> /usr/src/linux
$ cd /usr/src/linux
$ cp /boot/config-<version> .config
$ make oldconfig
$ make menuconfig
$ make-kpkg clean
$ make-kpkg --rootcmd fakeroot kernel_image \
            --revision <rev> --initrd
```

I can install the newly built kernel package with dpkg.

---

[2] http://www.kernel.org/

## Compiling kernel modules

For some modules, which aren't in the Debian kernel and not in the kernel from www.kernel.org, there are prepared package whose name usually ends in *-source* (for instance *squashfs-source* with Debian 5 or *openswan-modules-source* with Debian 6). I can install these packages and then compile the modules using *module-assistant*:

```
$ sudo apt-get install module-assistant
$ sudo apt-get install openswan-modules-source
$ sudo m-a build openswan-modules
$ sudo dpkg -i /usr/src/openswan-modules-$version.deb
$ sudo modprobe ipsec
```

Details can be found on the manual pages.

# Software for OpenWrt

I don't have to go out of my way to compile software for OpenWrt on ALIX devices. Because the computer works with X86 CPU I don't need a cross compiler. I only have to take the installed libraries into account and, if necessary recompile my program with these libraries.

OpenWrt's documentation wiki[3] is the first place to look for answers to questions regarding self-compiled software. If I don't find an answer there, I can search for an answer in the Forum[4] or pose the question myself.

---
[3] http://wiki.openwrt.org/
[4] http://forum.openwrt.org/

# Daily operation and administration

Once I have installed Linux and the necessary software on my ALIX computer I have to give some thought to its operation. How do I configure the computer for the network, how do I update the software and how do I tell if there is any updated software and whether I should install it or not.

## Configuring the computer for its intended use

In an ideal world I would not have to configure anything at all. Everything would be configured externally, for instance in the network using DHCP, Bonjour, Zero Configuration Networking or IPv6 auto configuration. I can do this for a streaming music client that is configured from the network and whose playlists are on the server. Plug it in, switch it on, it works.

That would be nice but life isn't always like that. The alternative is to configure the software on the device and - to make the configuration survive the next reboot - write it to a suitable medium. This medium, in the simplest case the root file system, must be writable at least during configuration. To make the root file system writable the scripts *remountrw* and *remountro* can be used which do exactly this, remount the root file system read-write ore read-only. Now I can write to the file system and can configure the device.

> **Tip**
>
> For the curious:
>
> ```
> mount -o remount,rw /
> ```
>
> and:
>
> ```
> mount -o remount,ro /
> ```
>
> do the same.

Because a Linux system contains software of diverse origin, configuration is also heterogeneous. The only common feature that nearly every type of software on Linux and UNIX has, is that text files can be configured using any text editor - traditionally vi. Even this common denominator starts to weaken since programs like Samba can be configured using a binary registry that is accessed using the *net* command.

Differences already crop up with the syntax of the configuration files. The key-value-pairs are sometimes separated by equal sign (=) and sometimes not. The configuration file may be divided into sections or it may contain complex block structures with brackets, parenthesis or other constructs. Some software provides the full range of the scripting language which it is written in in the configuration file. Other software uses different syntax in different files - ISC BIND to mention one.

There are even different ways of commenting on something in the configuration files, making the handbook or other documentation indispensable.

In truth there are projects that unite the configuration of the whole system or at least bring it under a consistent interface, like for instance *Webmin*, the somewhat out-of-date *linuxconf*, *UCI* from OpenWrt or the various server configuration programs. But with these I have to ask myself - particularly with regard to limited resources:

- Can I configure everything that needs to be configured with it?
- Do I have enough disk space and memory for the configuration program?
- Is it reasonably secure?
- Does it work with the read-only root file system?

In particular the last consideration would mean abandoning most of these programs.

So in most cases I have to resort to the traditional method of configuring directly in the text files that are used to configure my software, or software I've programmed myself, that acts like UCI, or a configuration management system like *cfengine*, *chef* or *puppet* if I use these in the remaining network as well.

## Configuration with UCI from OpenWrT

The *Unified Configuration Interface* (UCI) from the OpenWrt project is an interesting approach. Because ALIX computers have been able to use OpenWrt since the *Kamikaze* version, I can test its advantages configuring computers using CompactFlash as a permanent storage medium.

UCI can stand alone and can be adapted to other distributions, but it takes some time to make it work. There is a note regarding this on the OpenWrt web page.

The main configuration of OpenWrt is under */etc/config/*. In this directory you will find text files for every part of the system that needs to be configured. These files can be modified with an editor, the command line program *uci* or with one of the different programming interfaces (Shell, Lua, C). The web interface *LuCI* is based directly on the programming interface.

## The graphical interface LuCI from OpenWrt

One advantage of the web administration interface LuCI is that it makes the administration of the device acceptable for people who would rather avoid the command line. With some knowledge of the programming language Lua, I can enhance this interface to meet my requirements.

For instance, I had the system partition remounted read-only on an ALIX computer with OpenWrt and *ext2* file system and added two scripts so that I could switch easily between read-write and read-only. In order to use the same functionality with the web interface I used the extension described in chapter four.

# The iptables firewall on OpenWrt

If I want to deploy OpenWrt on my computer and use the packet filter firewall it would be best to understand the context, especially if I want to use the command line tool *uci* or the web interface *LuCI* in the configuration.

Indeed it is possible to override all of the settings of the configuration interface in the file */etc/firewall.user*, but then I would miss out on all the advantages of structuring using the web interface.

## The model

The iptables rules are distributed over the different chains in a defined plan on OpenWrt. Knowledge of this plan helps to understand and be able to analyze the filter rules.

The firewall is basically divided into zones such as *wan* and *lan*. For each of these zones there is a set of rule chains which are linked according to the firewall configuration settings. These links for the different firewall tables (*filter*, *mangle*, *nat* and *raw*) are illustrated in the following model.

The *filter* table contains all of the rules which allow or deny the passage of data packets. The model for it looks like this:

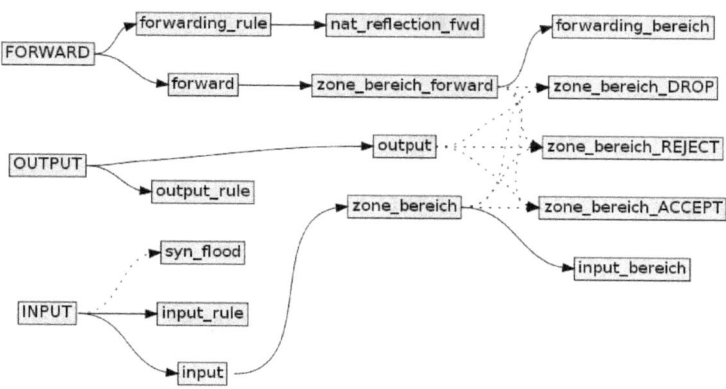

Model of the filter rules

In this diagram the word *bereich* in the name of a rule chain stands for one of the zones defined in UCI. That means if I defined the zones *lan* and *wan*, there are rule chains named zone_lan, zone_wan, zone_lan_ACCEPT, zone_wan_ACCEPT, zone_lan_DROP, zone_wan_DROP etc.

In the model, solid lines represent fixed jump targets. Dotted lines stand for jump targets which may or may not exist depending on the configuration settings.

A jump from one zone rule chains to another can occur between different chains depending on the settings. For example, a jump from rule chain zone_lan_forward to chain zone_wan_ACCEPT occurs if data transit from zone *lan* to zone *wan* is allowed.

The jump from chain INPUT to chain syn_flood depends on whether the setting *Enable SYN-flood protection* is enabled in the configuration settings or not.

It is important to keep in mind that this model doesn't reveal the order of the jumps between the chains. To find out this information you would need a more detailed visualization of the firewall rules.

The model for the *nat* table is more straightforward:

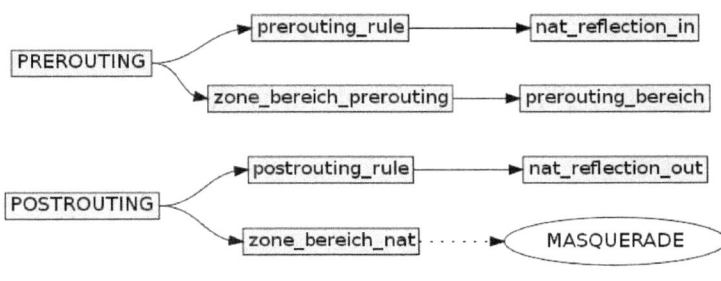

Model of the nat rules

Even easier are the models for the tables *mangle*

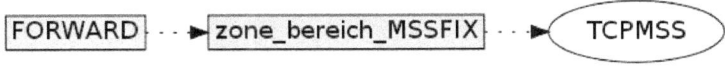

Model of the mangle rules

and *raw*:

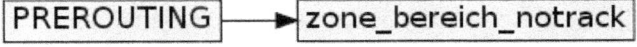

Model of the raw rules

This gives you an idea about the basic relationship between the rule chains. Now I'll go into detail about configuration.

## Common settings

Before I come to the actual firewall settings I will digress briefly and talk about the network settings. You'll find these under **Network -> Interfaces** with LuCI and in the file */etc/config/network* with UCI. Or I can use the command uci show network to display them. Data about the actual state of the network, for instance settings derived from DHCP, can be found in */var/state/network*. I obtain these in the command line interface with:

```
# uci -P /var/state show network
```

With LuCI I can assign every interface to a firewall zone under the interface's *Firewall Settings* tab. These settings correspondend with the settings under **Network -> Firewall** for the zone in question (under *Covered Networks*).

With UCI the networks are specified in *firewall.@zone[x].network* as a space separated list. I add them in the command line interface with the command uci add_list:

```
...
# uci add_list firewall.@zone[-1].network=lan1
# uci add_list firewall.@zone[-1].network=lan2
...
```

Thus the symbolic network names (*lan, wan*) are used as values and not the names of the physical interfaces.

## Common firewall settings

I can find the common firewall settings in the upper area of the page **Network->Firewall**. Here we have the tabs *General Settings* and *Custom Rules*.

The latter enables the file */etc/firewall.user* to be customized within the web interface. This file is a shell script which is called up after configuration in accordance with the input given to LuCI or UCI. Because it is a shell script, all of the firewall rules have to be initiated with iptables, the program which sets the rules in the kernel, and they have to adhere to the syntax understood by this program. In UCI there is only a reference to the name of this script in the variable *firewall.@include[0]*.

Now let's return to the common settings.

| General Settings | Custom Rules | |
|---|---|---|
| Enable SYN-flood protection | ☑ | |
| Drop invalid packets | ☑ | |
| Input | accept | |
| Output | accept | |
| Forward | reject | |

General firewall settings

A check mark after *Enable SYN-flood protection* corresponds to the entry *firewall.@default[0].syn_flood=1* in UCI and creates the rule chain *syn_flood* in the *filter* table. There is a jump from the *INPUT* rule chain to this chain for TCP packets which have set the FIN-, SYN-, RST- or SYN-ACK-bit. The *syn_flood* chain contains a rule which limits the number of such packets per time unit and otherwise jumps back to the normal rule evaluation.

A check mark after *Drop invalid packets* in LuCI corresponds to the entry *firewall.@default[0].drop_invalid=1* in UCI and creates a rule to discard invalid packets at the beginning of the *INPUT* chain.

In LuCI I can choose between an ACCEPT, DROP or REJECT policy for the chains *INPUT, OUTPUT* and *FORWARD*.

The information in the LuCI illustration above corresponds to the following entries in UCI:

```
# uci set firewall.@defaults[0].syn_flood=1
# uci set firewall.@defaults[0].input=ACCEPT
# uci set firewall.@defaults[0].output=ACCEPT
# uci set firewall.@defaults[0].forward=REJECT
# uci set firewall.@defaults[0].drop_invalid=1
```

## Firewall zones

The zone settings in LuCI can be found in the middle area under **Network->Firewall**. These correspond to the section *firewall.@zone[x]* in UCI, whereby *x* is the index of the zone (beginning with 0). A value of -1 for *x* always denotes the latest zone (i.e. the one just created).

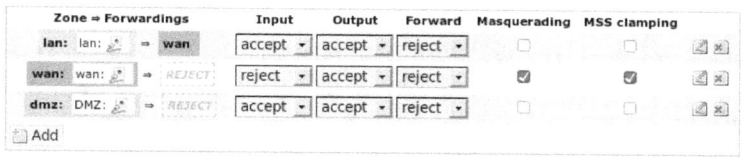

All firewall zones

The lower left button *Add* enables me to create a new zone in LuCI. Using UCI I would write:

```
# uci add firewall zone
# uci set firewall.@zone[-1].name=lan
# uci set firewall.@zone[-1].network=lan
# uci set firewall.@zone[-1].input=ACCEPT
# uci set firewall.@zone[-1].output=ACCEPT
# uci set firewall.@zone[-1].forward=REJECT
```

The name is used to specify some of the iptables rule chains. Therefore it should not contain special characters.

For every zone I can determine distinct policies for input, output and forward. In practice this means that there will be a jump to the zone_lan_ACCEPT chain at the end of the zone_lan chain since I have set the input policy for zone *lan* to ACCEPT (for more details please see the model of the *filter* table above). Additionally jumps are inserted from output to zone_lan_ACCEPT and from zone_lan_forward to zone_lan_REJECT. The reason why these jumps don't go to the standard targets *ACCEPT*, *DROP* or *REJECT*, is that this way the policies are restricted to the corresponding zone.

This section defines common properties of "lan". The *input* and *output* options set the default policies for traffic entering and leaving this zone while the *forward* option describes the policy for forwarded traffic between different networks within the zone. *Covered networks* specifies which available networks are member of this zone.

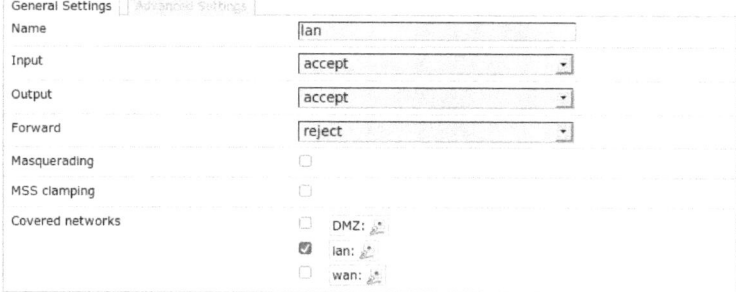

General firewall zone settings

A check mark after *Masquerading* corresponds to *firewall.@zone[-1].masq=1* and creates a jump to *MASQUERADE* in the zone_-$zone_nat rule chain. This effectively switches on masquerading for this zone which hides all addresses behind the address of the router.

A check mark after *MSS clamping* corresponds to *firewall.@zone[-1].mtu_fix=1* and creates a rule chain which restricts the maximum segment size (MSS) for tcp and is called zone_$zone_-MSSFIX in the *mangle* table. This is important, for instance, at the PPPoE interfaces of DSL routers to ensure that the path MTU of the TCP connections which run through this interface is set up correctly.

I can choose which networks should belong to this zone in the area *Covered networks*. This corresponds to the firewall settings under **Network->Interface** in LuCI. I add these settings in UCI like this:

```
# uci add_list firewall.@zone[-1].network=lan
```

| General Settings | Advanced Settings | |
|---|---|---|
| Restrict to address family | IPv4 and IPv6 | |
| Restrict Masquerading to given source subnets | | |
| Restrict Masquerading to given destination subnets | | |
| Force connection tracking | ☐ | |
| Enable logging on this zone | ☐ | |

Advanced firewall zone settings

Under *Advanced Settings* I can restrict the zone to one address family (IPv4, IPv6) or I can allow both. In UCI this corresponds to firewall.@zone[-1]=ipv4 for IPv4 and ipv6 for IPv6. I omit this line if I want to allow both.

If I have enabled masquerading, I can restrict it here to one or more source networks and/or one or more destination networks. The corresponding settings in UCI are:

```
# uci add_list firewall.@zone[-1].masq_src=1.2.3.4/24
# uci add_list firewall.@zone[-1].masq_src=1.2.3.4/24
# uci add_list firewall.@zone[-1].masq_dest=5.6.7.8/24
```

The associated firewall rules appear in the chain zone_$zone_nat in the *nat* table. If I have declared multiple networks, there will be a rule for each pair of source and destination networks.

Connection tracking is disabled per default in the OpenWrt firewall if no masquerading is activated. For this purpose NOTRACK rules are inserted that incorporate all of the traffic in the zone. This takes pressure of the router but masquerading does not work without connection tracking.

If I do want connection tracking even when no masquerading is in use, I can switch it on with *Force connection tracking*. Or in UCI:

```
# uci set firewall.@zone[-1].conntrack=1
```

I can switch on logging with *Enable logging on this zone* and then limit the number of log messages per time unit with *Limit log messages*. In UCI:

```
# uci set firewall.@zone[-1].log=1
# uci set firewall.@zone[-1].log_limit=20/minute
```

## Forwarding

If I run an NAT router and want to forward incoming traffic to an internal computer (for instance for remote access or some online games), I must select the computer to which the traffic should be forwarded beforehand.

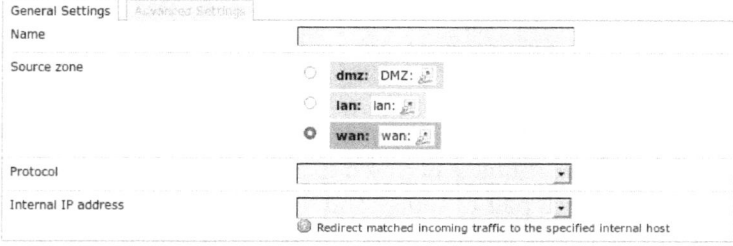

Redirection general settings

I set this up in the area *Redirections* on the page **Network->Firewall**. The *Add* button enables me to create a new redirection. In UCI:

```
# uci firewall add redirect
# uci set firewall.@redirect[-1]._name=SSH
# uci set firewall.@redirect[-1].src=wan
# uci set firewall.@redirect[-1].proto=tcp
# uci set firewall.@redirect[-1].src_dport=2222
# uci set firewall.@redirect[-1].dest=lan
# uci set firewall.@redirect[-1].dest_ip=1.2.3.4
# uci set firewall.@redirect[-1].dest_port=22
# uci set firewall.@redirect[-1].target=DNAT
```

*Name* is only for commenting purposes.

*Source zone* in LuCI denotes the zone for which the forwarding applies (in UCI `src`). This is usually the *wan* zone because there you often have masquerading set to on.

Next I choose the *Protocol* (UCI: `proto`) to be forwarded. LuCI allows me to choose between *TCP+UDP*, *TCP*, *UDP* and *custom*. The first three correspond to `tcpudp`, `tcp` and `udp` in UCI. If I select these in LuCI the page changes and I can choose the port on the interface (*External port*) and at the target computer (*Internal port*). In UCI I specify `src_port` and `dest_port` respectively. If both ports are the same I can choose the value 0-65535 for *Internal port* in LuCI or omit `dest_port` in UCI.

In LuCI the internal computer is specified with *Internal IP address* and in UCI with `dest_ip`.

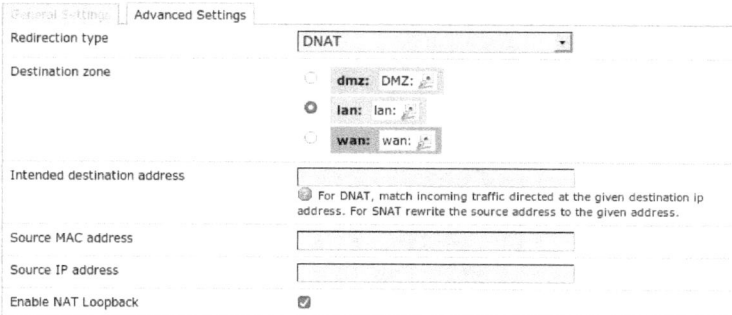

Redirection advanced settings

Under *Advanced Settings* in LuCI I can choose between the *Redirection Type* DNAT and SNAT (in UCI: target).

*Destination zone* allows me to specify the zone where the target computer is connected (UCI: dest).

These two settings and a check mark next to *Enable NAT Loopback* (UCI: reflection, here 0 means deactivate it) enable me to determine the number and the meaning of the rules which are created.

With DNAT three rules are created in the *nat* table:

- In the zone_$zone_prerouting rule chain all of the connections are redirected to the target computer in the internal network.
- In the nat_reflection chain all of the connections from the destination zone that are trying to reach the combination external address/external port are redirected to the internal address/internal port.
- In the nat_reflection_out chain the source address is changed to the address of the router in the target network

for all of the connections from the destination zone to the target computer/target port.

The first rule is obvious and applies to all connections from the outside. The second and third rules are necessary to allow me to reach the target computer from the internal network with the same combination of address and port as is used from the outside. This only works if the router gets the response packets from the target host too so that it can modify the addresses in all of the data packets. These last two rules are only generated if I check *Enable NAT Loopback* in LuCI or if `firewall.@redirect[-1].reflection=0` is omitted in UCI.

With SNAT (in *Advanced Settings*) LuCI will only create one rule in the zone_$zone_nat chain from the *nat* table for the zone of the destination network. If a matching packet passes the router, the source address changes.

*Intended destination address* (UCI: `src_dip`) has a double meaning according to the setting in *Redirection type*: With DNAT the rule is only followed if the destination address of the packet matches. With SNAT the source address is changed to the specified address. This makes sense if the masquerading interface has more than one IP address.

*Source MAC address, Source IP address, Source port* (UCI `src_mac`, `src_ip`, `src_port`) enable me to further restrict the matching data packets.

## Rules

I specify the firewall rules in the lower part (*Rules*) of the page **Network->Firewall** in LuCI.

**General rule settings**

With UCI:

```
# uci add firewall rule
# uci set firewall.@rule[-1].src=wan
# uci set firewall.@rule[-1].target=ACCEPT
# uci set firewall.@rule[-1].proto=udp
# uci set firewall.@rule[-1].dest_port=68
```

*Name* (UCI: _name) is optional and is only for commenting purposes.

*Source_zone* (UCI: src) determines the rule chain in the *filter* table where the rules will be written. See the model introduced above for further context.

*Protocol, Source address, port, Destination address, port* and *Action* (UCI: proto, src_ip, src_port, dest_ip, dest_port, target) determine the parameters of the rule. In LuCI some parameters are hidden or enabled according to the selected protocol. For instance the ports only make sense for TCP and UDP and *icmp_type* is only relevant for ICMP.

Advanced rule settings

I can specify the rules even further within the *Advanced settings*.

Using *Destination zone* (UCI: dest) I can determine that a rule shall only apply to packets destined for a certain zone. In this case the rule does not end with a jump to one of the standard targets (ACCEPT, DROP, REJECT) but instead goes to zone_$dest_ACCEPT, zone_$dest_DROP and zone_$dest_REJECT accordingly so that datagrams for other zones won't be affected by this rule.

Using *Source MAC address* (UCI: src_mac) I can define that the rule only be valid for a certain device, even if it obtains different IP addresses from DHCP.

Finally I can restrict the rule to IPv4 or IPv6 with *Restrict to address family* (UCI: family).

This completes our excursion into the configuration of the packet firewall on OpenWrt.

## Updates

Updating is relatively easy when I have mounted the root partition read-write. I use the packet manager to do this:

```
# remountrw
# apt-get update && apt-get dist-upgrade
# remountro
```

And accordingly with OpenWrt:

```
# remountrw
# opkg update
# opkg list-upgradable
# opkg upgrade <pkgs>
# remountro
```

With software I've compiled myself I just copy the new version to */usr/local/stow* and change the symbolic links to the new version with *stow*:

```
$ sudo remountrw
$ ./configure --prefix /usr/local/stow/monotone-1.0
...
$ sudo make install
$ sudo stow -D -d /usr/local/stow monotone-0.99.1
$ sudo stow -d /usr/local/stow monotone-1.0
$ sudo remountro
```

After I have assured myself that the new version works, I remove the directory of the old version.

Security updates could be a problem. With Debian I can get these automatically. But I have to call up `apt-get update` regularly. There are software packages like *apticron* or *cron-apt* which do this automatically and according to schedule by *cron*. But the files and directories under */var/cache/apt* must be writable to do this. Furthermore a sendmail (for instance from the package *nullmailer*) must be installed and configured because these programs use email to report available software updates.

Alternatively I can just get the list of the installed software including its installed versions and compare this list on another computer with the current versions of the software.

In any event when I use self-compiled software I must look out myself for newer versions.

## Backup and Restore

Because the configuration of the device usually doesn't change very often after deployment, it seldom has to be backed up. In most cases I just have to backup the configuration as long as I have not installed any new software, have not removed anything and have not updated the software.

After an update or after installing or removing software I like to do a full backup to quickly restore the device to this state. To do this I recommend an approach that should work on all devices regardless which distribution is installed. First I determine the device file of the CF card. Usually this should be */dev/hda* or */dev/sda* depending on the kernel and kernel module (see the section about the kernel in Chapter 6 for details). Then I can read the whole CF card with the *dd* program and write it to a file on another computer.

```
$ ssh root@192.168.1.1 dd if=/dev/sda \
| dd of=router.img
```

I redirect the output of *dd* into an image file which I later can write unchanged to another CF card of at least the same size.

On systems with two root partitions of the same size (for example Voyage Linux installed with *pxe-initrd*) I can write the content of the active and mounted read-only root partition to the other partition using a script. If the root partition has gotten mixed up in an upgrade, I can boot from the second root partition and copy it back to the first root partition. Of course I need access to the serial console for this to work. But then I can repair a not-so-successful update fast. However this does not do away with the fact that I have a defective CF card so I need the full backup mentioned in the previous paragraph anyway.

## OpenWrt

OpenWrt provides some simple means for backup using UCI. I can get the current configuration in machine readable form in the command line using:

```
# uci export
```

I pick up this configuration with SSH and write it to a file on another machine. Since it is plain text I can use a version control system to track changes. To restore the configuration on a new machine I call up:

```
# uci import
```

The passwords, however, are not included in the saved configuration. For these I must additionally save the file */etc/passwd*.

# Strategies for problem solving

In this chapter I'll go into detail about some of the strategies I have used in the past to solve problems.

## Manual pages, program documentation

There are many places I can turn to for help. Usually one of the first is the manual pages and other program documentation. With Debian I use `dpkg -L` to obtain a list of all files belonging to a package. Manual pages are located under */usr/share/man*. More information can often be found under */usr/share/doc/packagename*. Here I look for files whose name starts with *README*. Sometimes there is a package named *packagename-doc* which contains further documentation for *packagename*. For self compiled software I can look in the source archives.

There is also a program called *apropos* which lets you search for keywords in the descriptions of the manual pages. I can use the slash (/) to search on a manual page.

In documentation directories I use `grep -ri` to search.

Unfortunately this won't help if I have removed nearly all documentation due to a shortage of space.

## Internet, search engines

Another easy strategy which I also often use as a starting point is to search the internet. Often someone else has had the same problem and has perhaps even found a solution to it - which is even better. I limit myself to about 10 to 15 minutes when looking in the internet for a solution. Here I have to narrow the problem down to generate appropriate search words. I often find the necessary information in the system logs.

I look for keywords in those log lines which point to the problem and copy them to the search form in the browser. Often I take the whole line and just remove the parts that are probably different on other machines (date, pid, computer name, addresses, ...). I look in the results to see whether these describe my problem or - even better - contain a solution. If I get too many results, I look at those that come closest to my problem for further keywords. It's great when I am able to solve my problem. I note it down in my journal and then get on with my day.

For example I found the following log line on one of my routers:

```
Dec  5 05:17:01 baas authpriv.err CRON[17414]: \
pam_env(cron:session): Unable to open env file: \
/etc/default/locale: No such file or directory
```

Hence I used the following keywords for the internet search:

```
authpriv CRON pam_env "Unable to open env file" \
"No such file or directory"
```

I didn't come up with much using Google I but DuckDuckGo gave me information about Debian bug #442049 among other things. I entered this number to the bug database[5]. The solution in this case was easy. The missing file */etc/default/locale* belonged to a *locales* package which wasn't used on the router. *Pam_env* was trying to access this file without checking its existence. The workaround:

```
# touch /etc/default/locale
```

If I can't find a solution in the manual pages or through an internet search, I try to solve the problem alone or at least to narrow it down so that I can ask a specific question in one of the support forums. Here I proceed differently depending on whether I suspect the problem to be more on the local machine or on the network.

## Strategies for local problems on the computer

When the problem is that a program doesn't work correctly or even at all, I have to observe what it's doing in the first place. I have already looked in the system logs and maybe have an idea of what may be the cause.

If I suspect a problem with a shell script, I can start it with `sh -x scriptname` and get more information about the sequence of actions. This may already help or point me towards another program that I should be looking closer at.

---

[5] http://bugs.debian.org/44209

For problems with Perl programs I can use `perl -d scriptname` to start the Perl debugger. This requires at least a basic knowledge of this program language and the Perl debugger.

> **Tip**
>
> The manual pages of Unix and Linux systems are traditionally grouped in sections. Popular sections are
>
> 1 for executable programs
>
> 2 for system calls
>
> 3 for library functions
>
> 5 for file formats
>
> 8 for executable programs for system administration
>
> If there are manual pages with the same name in different sections, man selects any one of these. To get a page from a specific section I put the section before the name of the page:
>
> ```
> $ man 2 open
> ```
>
> If I want to look at all of the pages with the same name, I can use the option `-a`:
>
> ```
> $ man -a open
> ```

When I come across a binary program (ELF executable), I can use *strace* to get an overview of the system calls. To do this I start strace with the command line `strace -f -o xyz.strace` `programname` or `strace -f -o xyz.strace -p pid` if the program is already running and has *pid* as its process id. Then I find the system calls of the program in the text file *xyz.strace* and may already see the cause of the problem. If the program generates error messages, I search for these messages in *xyz.strace* and see what has happened immediately before this. This method allows me to easily localize problems with access rights. Of course I need to have knowledge about the system calls which I can find in section two of the manual pages.

If a program crashes, I can try to produce a core dump and analyze this with a debugger. To do this I must tell the system to write a core dump when a program crashes:

```
$ ulimit -c 1000000
```

Here the option `-c 1000000` indicates the maximum size of the core dump file that should be written. The exact meaning of this command is in the man page of the shell (for instance `man bash` and then search for *ulimit*).

If I want information about running programs, I can use *lsof*, *strace* and *fuser* depending on the kind of information I want to get.

If I suspect missing or false libraries, I can get help from *ldd*.

## Troubleshooting mount problems

The following example for the localization of a problem with the read-only mount of the root partition is taken from a real case and should clarify the procedure.

On the computer in question I noticed the following line on the console:

```
Remounting / as read-only ... mount: / is busy
```

After logging in I could verify this with:

```
# mount
...
/dev/hda2 on / type ext2 (rw,noatime,errors=continue)
...
# remountro
mount: / is busy
```

This was not what I wanted for this machine. So I had to find out which processes prevented the read-only mount. For the most part these are processes which had opened a file to write on the partition in question. I used the program *fuser* to find out which processes:

```
# fuser -vm /
                     USER          PID ACCESS COMMAND
/:                   root          kernel mount /
...
                     root          1467 Frce. dhclient
...
```

In this case it was only one process and it had the file still open. I could verify this by stopping the process and then remounting the root partition to read-only using *remountro*.

The next step was to find out which file this process kept open, so that I could move this file to some other place if necessary. The program *lsof* helped me do this:

```
# lsof -p 1431
COMMAND   PID USER  FD   TYPE..NAME
dhclient 1431 root  cwd  DIR../
dhclient 1431 root  rtd  DIR../
dhclient 1431 root  txt  REG../sbin/dhclient
dhclient 1431 root  mem  REG../lib/libnss_files-...
dhclient 1431 root  mem  REG../lib/libc-2.11.2.so
dhclient 1431 root  mem  REG../lib/ld-2.11.2.so
dhclient 1431 root   0u  CHR../dev/null
dhclient 1431 root   1u  CHR../dev/null
dhclient 1431 root   2u  CHR../dev/null
dhclient 1431 root   3w  REG../var/lib/dhcp/dhclient\
.eth0.leases
dhclient 1431 root   4u  pack..type=SOCK_PACKET
dhclient 1431 root   5u  IPv4..*:bootpc
```

I had restarted the computer to restore the same conditions and this time the *dhclient* process had the PID 1431. The process kept */var/lib/dhcp/dhclient.eth0.lease* open for writing. Thus this file had to be moved to another place.

I first tried adding */var/lib/dhcp* to the variable *VOYAGE_SYNC_DIRS* in the file */etc/default/voyage-util*. Unfortunately this didn't work:

```
# mount
...
/dev/hda2 on / type ext2 (rw,noatime,errors=continue)
...
tmpfs on /var/lib/dhcp type tmpfs (rw,no...,mode=755)
# fuser -vm /
...
                    root      1440 Frce. dhclient
...
# lsof -p 1440
COMMAND   PID USER  FD TYPE..NAME
dhclient 1440 root cwd  DIR../
...
dhclient 1440 root  3w REG../var/lib/dhcp/dhclien...
```

The file *dhclient.eth0.leases* was still open in the root partition even though it's path referred to another file system. In this case it turned out that a race condition caused the DHCP client to open the file before */var/lib/dhcp* was mounted as a tmpfs. The ultimate solution was to make sure the network was initialized after *voyage-sync* was executed.

Later I found out that with Voyage Linux */var/lib/dhcp* is actually a link to */lib/init/rw/var/lib/dhcp* and the tmpfs under */lib/init/rw* is setup much earlier. I don't know why it wasn't the case with this machine.

## Strategies for network problems

A very good book for troubleshooting network problems is **Network Troubleshooting Tools** by *Joseph D. Sloan*.

I divide problems in the network arbitrarily into completely defective connections, partially defective connections and random dropouts / performance problems. I check flaws in this order too.

First of all I check whether there is any connection between the affected systems. I can use *ping*, for example to make an initial decision.

If this doesn't prove fruitful, I check whether the addresses of both systems are set correctly in terms of the network and if there are routes to the respective network in case both machines are not on the same network segment. The programs *netstat*, *ifconfig*, *ip*, *route* and *arp* help me do this:

```
$ /sbin/ifconfig
...
eth0      Link encap:Ethernet   HWaddr 00:0d:b9:21:...
          inet addr:192.168.1.254  Bcast:192.168.1...
          inet6 addr: fe80::20d:b9ff:fe21:715c/64 ...
          UP BROADCAST RUNNING MULTICAST MTU:1500 ...
          RX packets:1755606 errors:0 dropped:75 o...
          TX packets:2584367 errors:0 dropped:0 ov...
          collisions:0 txqueuelen:1000
          RX bytes:212300464 (202.4 MiB) TX bytes:...
          Interrupt:10 Base address:0xc000
...
$ ip addr show
...
2: eth0: <BROADCAST,MULTICAST,UP,LOWER_UP> mtu 150...
    link/ether 00:0d:b9:21:71:5c brd ff:ff:ff:ff:f...
    inet 192.168.1.254/24 brd 192.168.1.255 scope ...
    inet6 fe80::20d:b9ff:fe21:715c/64 scope link
```

```
            valid_lft forever preferred_lft forever
...
```

The output from *ip* is shorter but contains the information necessary to obtain a diagnosis so I prefer this tool. It shows me the ip address, network mask and ethernet MAC address. *arp* enables me to see whether the address of the computer is added to the ARP cache:

```
$ ping 192.168.1.254
$ /usr/sbin/arp -n 192.168.1.254
Address         HWtype HWaddress           Flags Mask Iface
192.168.1.254 ether 00:0d:b9:21:71:5c C                eth0
```

If ping does not work but the MAC address appears in the ARP cache, this points to a host firewall suppressing PING messages.

If the connection encompasses different networks I first use *ping* to see whether I can reach the gateway to the other network. I determine the gateway using `netstat -r` (or `route` which delivers the same output) or `ip route show`:

```
$ netstat -rn
Kernel-IP-Routentabelle
Ziel            Router              Genmask         Flags MSS ...
192.168.1.0 0.0.0.0                 255.255.255.0   U     0 ...
0.0.0.0         192.168.1.254 0.0.0.0               UG    0 ...
$ ip route show
192.168.1.0/24 dev eth0 proto kernel scope link sr...
default via 192.168.1.254 dev eth0
```

If the connection runs through several networks I can try to discover the path using *traceroute*. Here I have to remember that traceroute may be disrupted by packet filters which suppress ICMP messages, or by NAT. If you keep this in mind, *traceroute* can sometimes help localize the fault location.

If the addresses and routes are configured correctly and the gateways - if necessary - reachable, I get out the big gun and monitor the line on both ends to see whether the datagrams are being sent and received at all. I use *tcpdump* and/or *wireshark* to do this.

If I see more datagrams on one computer than on the other, I can act on the assumption that there are packet drops or a firewall in the network. Then I can leave both computers as they are and turn my attention to the network.

If I see the same datagrams on both computers but one does not send, I can assume that there is a packet filter on that computer. This can be verified and corrected with *iptables*.

If I get a connection with PING between two computers, this need not imply that I can reach the service that I want to use.

For security reasons many services are bound to the loopback interface (address 127.0.0.1) after installation and are therefore not available through the network. I can use `netstat -ntl` for TCP services and `netstat -aun` for UDP services to verify this. Here I should see the external IP address or 0.0.0.0 in the column *Local Address*, followed by a colon (:) and the port number of the service. If I don't see this, I must look in the configuration of the service. If the service is bound to the external interface and still doesn't answer, I use *iptables* to see if there are any filter rules that prevent it from answering. If there are no filter rules I can look in the files */etc/hosts.allow* and */etc/hosts.deny*.

Finally I can monitor the network interface using *tcpdump* and see how the computer reacts to connection requests. *strace* allows me to see whether the datagrams arriving at the interface are handled by the right server process.

If I do have a connection to the service but there are performance problems or dropouts, then I must capture the whole session and analyze it with *wireshark*.

If I assume there are network problems, I can use `ping -f` or a program like *iperf* to do a performance test.

If I have eliminated all of the other problems so far and *tcpdump* is showing me that there is a connection to the service despite the error messages, I must analyze the protocol of the service. I can use the system logs together with a sufficient debugging level if the service supports this. Otherwise - with clear text protocols - I can look at the captured session with *wireshark* (Option *Follow TCP Stream*). With clear text protocols I can start a session manually with *netcat* or *telnet* and for SSL connections with *openssl*:

```
$ openssl s_client -connect webserver:443
```

A method for analyzing the TFTP protocol can be found in the section of this protocol in the chapter about protocols and mechanisms.

# Protocols and mechanisms

In this chapter I'll discuss some of the protocols and mechanisms that require at least a minimum of understanding.

## Bootloader

A bootloader is the first program that gets loaded by the firmware (the BIOS in IBM-compatible PCs) and executed. The bootloader then loads further parts of the operating system, usually the kernel.

Traditionally the bootloader consists of at least two parts: The first part (stage 1) is tiny and is placed in the master boot record (MBR) of the hard disk. Its job is to load the second part (stage 2) which often displays a menu for selecting the kernel and inputting additional kernel parameters and loads the selected kernel.

There are three main bootloaders for Linux on X86 systems: *LILO*, *GRUB* and *SYSLINUX*. Each one has its specific advantages and drawbacks and their suitability varies depending on the case of operation. Below I will go into a bit of detail about the three bootloaders.

### LILO

*Linux Loader* (LILO) is a well-proven bootloader for Linux. LILO is usually configured in the file */etc/lilo.conf*. Details can be found in the manual. In addition to Linux, LILO can load other operating systems through chain loading.

After changes have been made to the configuration or a kernel has been upgraded, the program */sbin/lilo* has to be called up because this boot loader can't deal with file systems. The program */sbin/lilo* determines which hard disk blocks are to be loaded by the bootloader. If I forget to call up */sbin/lilo*, LILO can't load the desired kernel and the system may become useless.

LILO's drawback is also its advantage because it means LILO is not limited to known file systems and can also load the kernel from unknown file systems as long as these are not compressed or encrypted.

## GRUB

The *Grand Unified Bootloader* (GRUB) was initially developed as part of the GNU Hurd Project. Because GRUB is more flexible and can deal with file systems - here it isn't necessary to run a program to determine the hard disk blocks after every kernel update - it has replaced LILO in many systems.

At the moment GRUB is being reworked. The new version is called *GRUB 2*, the old one *GRUB Legacy*.

In the old GRUB version there was a stage 1.5 between stage 1 and stage 2 which could read only one file system type. Stage 1.5 was located in the blocks between the MBR and the first partition. There, the appropriate version was installed for reading the file system containing stage 2.

In the new GRUB, stage 2 is divided into a kernel and loadable modules. The kernel only contains essential code for decompression, hard disk access, a shell and an ELF loader for modules. During installation the modules for the file system and the remaining components are appended to the kernel. Because it is compressed it usually fits in the area between the MBR and the first partition.

## SYSLINUX

The *SYSLINUX* project creates a series of lightweight bootloaders for IBM-compatible devices, in particular:

**SYSLINUX**
> for booting from FAT or NTFS file systems

**ISOLINUX**
> for booting from CD-ROM ISO 9660 file systems

**PXELINUX**
> for booting from a network server with a Preboot Execution Environment (PXE)

**EXTLINUX**
> for booting from Linux ext2, ext3 or btrfs file systems

**MEMDISK**
> for booting older operating systems like MS-DOS from these media

The use of *SYSLINUX* is recommended in these special situations. I'll go into detail about PXELINUX in the next section.

## Preboot Execution Environment (PXE)

Using PXE I can start a computer with software loaded from the network. The code that enables PXE boot is mostly located in the network interface of the computer but can also come from a floppy disk, an USB device or a CD-ROM. The computer uses this code to communicate with a DHCP server in order to get information about the network and the next server. Afterwards it communicates with a TFTP server to load the operating system.

First the computer uses DHCP to search for a PXE compatible redirection service to obtain a valid network configuration and to get information about available boot servers. When it has received this information it then contacts the boot server to load the Network Bootstrap Program (NBP) via TFTP. The NBP then takes control of the process.

A software suitable as NBP which I can use for my purposes is PXELINUX.

The DHCP configuration suitable for PXE boot with PXELINUX could look like this if I use the ISC DHCP server:

```
allow booting;
allow bootp;
group {
    next-server <TFTP server address>;
    filename "/pxelinux.0";
    host <hostname> {
        hardware ethernet <ethernet address>;
    }
}
```

This is only the part of the server configuration that is responsible for PXE boot. I group together all of the computers that use the same bootloader and use the MAC address to identify them. Here it is possible to assign fixed addresses in the block following *host* using `fixed-address <hostname>`.

## PXELINUX

PXELINUX is a component of the SYSLINUX project. Most Linux distributions contain SYSLINUX. I can find the documentation in the files *syslinux.txt* and *pxelinux.txt* which most often can be found under the directory */usr/shar/doc/syslinux* if the package is installed.

To use PXELINUX I copy the file *pxelinux.0*, which is part of the software package, onto a TFTP server and create a directory named *pxelinux.cfg/*. This directory will contain the configuration files for PXELINUX. The names of the configuration files depend on the MAC and IP address of the booting computer. PXELINUX looks for its configuration file in the *pxelinux.cfg/* directory in the following order:

- First it looks for a file with a name like the client UUID if such an UUID is provided from the PXE stack. The standard UUID format uses hexadecimal numbers with lower case letters as for instance b8945908-d6a6-41a9-611d-74a6ab80b83d.
- Next it looks for a file with a name pertaining to the type of hardware and hardware address (MAC), all in hexadecimal numbers with lower case letters which are separated by hyphens. Using an ethernet card with the

MAC address 00:0D:B9:22:7D:24 it would look for a file named 01-00-0d-b9-22-7d-24. Note the prepended string *01-*.
- Next it looks for a file with a name like the IPv4 address encoded as a hexadecimal number with upper case letters (For instance with IP address 192.168.1.5 it would look for a file named C0A80105). There is a program that is a component of SYSLINUS called *gethostip* which computes the hexadecimal number for any IP address.
- If there is no file with a name like the IP address in the previous step, it removes one hexadecimal number from the end of the name and tries again until it findes a file or until there is no hexadecimal number left in the name. Thus it is possible to use the same configuration file for just one IP address, sixteen addresses, 256, 4096, and so on, depending on the length of the file name.
- If it still hasn't found a file, it takes the file named *default* (in lower case) as a last resort.

Since version 3.20 PXELINUX restarts the computer after a timeout if a configuration file hasn't been found. Thus the computer remains active even when there are problems with the boot server.

PXELINUX needs a TFTP server which understands the *tsize* extension of the TFTP protocol. This could be *tftp-hpa* for instance.

The file *syslinux.txt* describes the directives available in the configuration file. The most important ones for PXELINUX are:

**LOCALBOOT 0**

with PXELINUX this means that the computer will boot

from the local disk instead of from a kernel loaded through the network. 0 means a normal system start.

I always write this into the *default* file to avoid accidental installation.

**SERIAL port [[baudrate**

flowcontrol]] opens the serial interface as a console. For ALIX computers this directive looks like this:

```
SERIAL 0 38400 0
```

**DEFAULT kernel options**

defines the kernel command line. This is used if PXELINUX starts automatically. It is possible to use a *label* here.

**LABEL label**

this entry is most often followed by a *KERNEL* entry which specifies the kernel and an *APPEND* entry which specifies the kernel command line.

I use the following entries, for instance, to install Linux via PXE boot on ALIX computers:

added line break for formatting
```
  serial 0 38400
  console 0
  label linux
    KERNEL vmlinuz
    APPEND initrd=initrd console=ttyS0,38400n1 \
           root=/dev/hda1
```

This means the files *vmlinuz* and *initrd* are on the same TFTP server.

## udev - managing devices dynamically

The Linux kernel uses *udev* to dynamically provide device files under */dev/*. Originally the directory */dev/* contained a fixed set of device files for all of the possible devices that may possibly be connected to the computer. Accordingly the directory was crowded and confusing and you didn't know if the file represented a device that was really connected until you tried it. Later *devfs* dynamically created device files under */dev/* for devices that were indeed connected to the computer. *Udev* is the current way of managing connected devices.

Hence *udev* relies on the information which the kernel provides via *sysfs* and the rules stipulated by the Linux distribution and the user of the computer. Thus it is possible to:

- rename device files

- assign alternate or persistent names for a device via symbolic links
- determine the name of a device file through the output of a program
- change the access rights and ownership of device files
- start a program if certain devices are connected to the computer
- rename network interfaces

## udev rules

Udev rules are read from files containing the suffix *.rules* in their names under the directories */lib/udev/rules.d/*, */etc/udev/rules.d/* and */dev/.udev/rules.d/* (for temporary rules). All rule files are sorted by name and processed in lexical order regardless of the directory they are in. File names must be unique: duplicate file names are ignored. Files under */etc/udev/rules.d/* take precedence over those under */lib/udev/rules.d/*. Thus it is possible to deactivate rule files under */lib/udev/rules.d/*.

In the rule files, blank lines and lines starting with # are ignored. All other lines are interpreted as rules. Every rule must be on it's own line and consist of one or more key-value pairs which are separated by a comma (,).

There are two kinds of keys: match and assignment. Once all of the match keys match their values, the assignment keys are assigned their value. The operator determines how matching and assignment are carried out. When writing my own rules I have to consult the *udev* manual page because some keys can be used for matching as well as for assignment (for instance *ATTR{key}* and *ENV{key}*).

I can use wild cards when matching. These have the following meaning:

\*         matches zero, one or more arbitrary characters.

?         matches exactly one arbitrary character.

[]        matches exactly one of the characters or character ranges given in the square bracket (for instance [0-9] matches any digit). If the first character between the brackets is an exclamation mark (!), it matches all characters which are not determined by this wild card.

Some of the assignment operators allow characters to be substituted in the rules. The complete list can be found on the manual page. Some important operators are:

*$kernel | %k*
: the kernel name for the device

*$number | %n*
: the kernel number for the device, for instance a partition number of a hard disk.

*$result | %c*
: the output of an external program

$$       the dollar sign itself

%%       the percent sign itself

## Information from sysfs

If I want to write udev rules, I try to describe the device as closely as possible. I can obtain the value of the different keys of a connected device using the *udevadm* program with the *info* command:

```
# udevadm info --query all --name /dev/ttyUSB0 \
         --attribute-walk
```

This command gives me all information about the device, which is at the moment accessible via */dev/ttyUSB0*, in order to identify it in my udev rules.

To get the information regarding a network card I use

```
# udevadm info --query all \
         --path /sys/class/net/eth0 \
         --attribute-walk
```

## Developing rules with udevadm

The program *udevadm* not only provides information about the connected devices, I can monitor udev for events like the connection or removal of a USB device, test the written rules and affect the status of the running udev process. More information is available on the manual page.

# DHCP

*Dynamic Host Configuration Protocol* (DHCP) is used to assign a network configuration to a client computer. The protocol is defined in RFC2131 and uses the UDP port 67 (for the server or relay agent) and 68 (for the client).

DHCP is an extension of the *Bootstrap Protocol* (BOOTP). It is widely compatible with the latter and can - with some limitations - work together with BOOTP clients and servers.

The client and server send different messages depending on the state of the client and the validity of its network information.

**DHCPDISCOVER**
> is sent by the client to the servers in the local network as a broadcast message.

**DHCPOFFER**
> is the response from the servers after getting a DHCPDISCOVER message from the client.

**DHCPREQUEST**
> is sent by the client to request one of the addresses offered by the servers. This message is also sent to ask the server for a renewal of the lease time for the requested address.

**DHCPACK**
> is the acknowledgement by the server of the address request sent by the client.

**DHCPNAK**
> is sent by the server if it refuses the request from the client.

**DHCPDECLINE**
> is sent by the client if the address offered by the server is already in use.

**DHCPRELEASE**
is sent by the client to release resources.

**DHCPINFORM**
is sent by the client for queries regarding data without IP addresses, for instance, because it has its address manually set.

The server may work in three different modes which influence the lease time of an address assignment.

Using *static allocation*, the mapping of IP addresses to MAC addresses is determined beforehand by the administrator.

With *automatic allocation* the DHCP server has an IP address range from which it permanently assigns addresses to client MAC addresses. If this range is completely used up, no further client can get an IP address from this server.

*Dynamic allocation* is like automatic allocation with the exception that an IP address is only assigned for a determined amount of time and the client has to renew the assignment in time. The time during which an assignment is valid is called *lease time*.

## Communication sequence

An **initial assignment** goes like this:

1. The client sends a UDP broadcast datagram with an DHCPRE-QUEST message from address 0.0.0.0:68 to address 255.255.255.255:67
2. One or more DHCP server send DHCPOFFER messages as a UDP broadcast to 255.255.255.255:68 with the source port 67.

3. The client chooses one of the offers and sends a DHCPRE-QUEST message to the chosen server. The server is identified through the server ID in the message. The other servers interpret this message as a rejection of their offers and can offer their addresses elsewhere.
4. The chosen server acknowledges its offer with more relevant data (DHCPACK) or it withdraws its offer (DHCP-NAK).
5. Before using the address, the client checks if it is already in use and if it is being used it rejects the address with DHCPDECLINE.

A **refresh with dynamic allocation** looks like this:

1. The client is told the lease time along with the IP address.
2. After half of the lease time has expired, the client sends a DHCPREQUEST message using unicast to the DHCP server to renew the lease.
3. When the server sends a DHCPACK message with a new lease time, the refresh is completed and the client can continuew using the address. After half of the lease time expires the client starts the next refresh.
4. If the server sends a DHCPNAK, the client must deactivate the use of the IP address on its network interface and begin a new initial assignment.
5. If the client doesn't receive an answer from the server after 7/8 of the lease time, it sends a DHCPREQUEST message as a broadcast to get a renewal from any server.
6. If the client could not renew its IP address at the end of the lease time, it must deactivate the use of the address and begin a new initial assignment.

## DHCP for different subnetworks

Remote networks may be connected to a DHCP server via DHCP relay agents. The relay agent receives the broadcast messages from the client and forwards them to the servers. The agent adds the IP address of the interface on which it received the broadcast to the datagram so that the server can determine the network for which the client should be configured. The relay agent receives the answer from the server at UDP port 67 and forwards it to the client's port 68.

## Security

DHCP is easy to disrupt since DHCP clients accept every DHCP server. If a foreign DHCP server is accidentally integrated into a network, the network can be paralyzed to a large extent.

An attacker can register all addresses of a DHCP server to prevent this server from responding to further requests (*DHCP Starvation Hack*). Afterwards the attacker can behave like a DHCP server.

When using DHCP in production networks, appropriate arrangements should be made like manageable switches and monitoring for unauthorized DHCP servers.

## IPv6

IPv6 does not need a DHCP service to configure network addresses. To distribute other information there is the protocol DHCPv6 which is specified in RFC3315 and does approximately the same for IPv6 as DHCPv4 does for IPv4. Unlike DHCPv4 the communication runs from UDP port 546 of the client to port 547 of the server.

# Trivial File Transfer Protocol (TFTP)

TFTP is a simple protocol for transferring files between computers. The protocol uses connection less protocols like UDP for file transfer. It is especially designed to load the operating system using firmware or small bootloaders and has the following characteristics:

- reading and writing files from or to a server
- **no** directory listings
- **no** authentication, compression or encryption

RFC1350 indicates the form of protocol that is currently being used. RFC2347 describes how to extend the protocol with options and RFC2349 indicates the transfer size option (*tsize*) needed for PXELINUX. This option enables the sending party to inform the receiving party of the size of the file to be transfered.

TFTP file transfer is always done between a client and a server and is initiated by the client. After a connection has been established this distinction is irrelevant for the protocol and it is more helpful to distinguish between sender and receiver. However a distinction between client and server is necessary for establishing the connection because it is only the server which waits for connections with a predetermined transfer identifier (TID). The TIDs of both partners are nothing more as the UDP ports in use and the server waits at UDP port 69 for connections.

## Establishing a connection

A client initiates a TFTP connection by sending a read request (RRQ) or write request (WRQ) and possibly some options to UDP port 69 of the server computer. The client's UDP port is selected randomly. The server determines a random UDP port for its side of this connection and sends the data to the client address and port. The server's initial may contain:

- an OACK message to accept or relay options
- an ACK message to accept the write request without options
- a message containing the first data block if the server sends the file but doesn't accept options
- an error message

Most error messages instantly close down the connection, details can be found in the referred to RFCs.

## Data transfer

When it comes to the actual data transfer it is more helpful to distinguish between sender and receiver because client and server behave exactly the same when they send or receive a file.

During data transfer the sender always sends one data packet with 512 bytes of data (unless there was a different block size negotiated when the connection was established as described in RFC2348) together with the respective block number. The receiver always answers with an acknowledgement message, which contains the same block number, or with an error message. If one message gets lost in transmission, the last message is retransmitted after a timeout.

Data transfer ends when a message with less data than the negotiated block size (or 512 bytes if nothing was negotiated) is sent. If the size of the file is an integer multiple of the block size, the sender must send a data message with 0 bytes of data to end the transfer. The transfer also ends when there is an error.

## Analyzing a TFTP session

When analyzing the protocol at network level with *tcpdump* or *wireshark* it is important to know that I can't easily filter the connection using ports. I must capture all of the UDP datagrams and possibly the ICMP messages between the two computers to analyze a TFTP session. One possible command line for *tcpdump* would be for instance:

```
# tcpdump -w tftp.pcap \
  \( icmp or udp \) and host client and host server
```

After finishing the capture I can determine the client's UDP port and use this knowledge to filter out the whole session:

```
# tcpdump -n -r tftp.pcap \
  host server and port 69
# tcpdump -nv -r tftp.pcap \
  host client and port clientport
```

If even the first datagram from the server is missing, an ICMP-Port-Unreachable datagram can signalize that there is no TFTP demon running on the server computer.

# Zero Configuration Networking

The origin of Zero Configuration Networking (Zeroconf) dates back to the 1990s. At that time Stuart Cheshire was working on networking computers using IP without explicit configuration. This technology has been integrated into Apple computers for some time now under the name *Rendezvous* and *Bonjour* respectively. It is available for Mac OSX, Windows, Linux, BSD UNIX and other operating systems. A very good book about Zeroconf is *Zero Configuration Networking / The Definitive Guide* by Stuart Cheshire and Daniel H. Steinberg.

From a technical standpoint Zeroconf is the combination of three technologies: *Dynamic Configuration of IPv4 Link-Local Addresses* (RFC3927), *Multicast-DNS* and *DNS Service Discovery*. The goal of Zeroconf is to make setting up a networking device as easy as turning on a table lamp: plug it in, switch it on, it works.

## Link local addressing

Every device in an IP network needs at least one unique IP address. If I operate my own network or connect to a professionally managed network, the address is either configured manually or provided through DHCP. Both methods require preparation work which I don't want to expend if I just want to temporary connect two laptops with an ethernet cable. This is precisely where I can use the automatic assignment of addresses according to RFC3927 for which the address range from 169.254.1.0 to 169.25.254.255 is reserved.

The procedure goes like this:

1. The computer chooses a random address in the mentioned range.
2. The computer sends ARP requests to find out whether another computer is already using this address. To do this it sets the sender IP address to 0.0.0.0 and the sender hardware address to its own hardware address.
3. a) If another computer claims the address by responding to the ARP request, the computer starts over from 1.

    b) If there is no response after a few seconds, the computer sends several ARP announcements to claim this address for itself and to clear possible stale entries for this address in the ARP caches of other computers.
4. If another computer tries to use this address at a later point in time, the computer defends the address by responding to the ARP requests.
5. If there are later conflicts, for instance because network segments which had been separated are then connected or because a rogue computer isn't playing by the rules, the standard requires the following: If a computer sees an ARP request for its own address from another computer, it sends, at most, one ARP response to raise its claim. If the other device doesn't give up the address, the computer has to abandon the use of the address and start over with 1.

## Multicast DNS

After getting an IP address for my computer I then need a name to refer to this IP address. To do this, I can use *Multicast DNS* (*mDNS*) if there is no configured DNS server.

There is no central authority within *mDNS*. Instead every client who wants to make a query sends its request through multicast to every interested machine in the network and responds when it sees a query for its own name.

Zeroconf uses the domain .local to distinguish between local names and existing domains. Like the addresses in the network 169.254/16, names in this domain are only unique in the local network. Names in this top level domain are usually resolved with *mDNS*. Every *mDNS* query is sent to multicast address 225.0.0.251 (FF02::FB with IPv6) and port 5353.

Multicast DNS identifies three categories of queries:

- one-shot queries
- one-shot queries that accumulate multiple responses
- continuous, ongoing queries

For one-shot queries where the client expects just one answer it only sends a DNS query to UDP port 5353 at address 224.0.0.251. This functionality is enough to resolve, for instance, http://some-name.local/ in a webbrowser.

With the second type of query the client knows that there may be multiple responses. It collects the responses and possibly repeats the query. With a repeated query it sends a list of already received responses so that these need not be sent another time. Follow-up queries are sent at a decreasing rate, in other words, with a growing interval between them.

Ongoing queries are used for instance for lists of available services. These queries are also sent at increasing intervals (up to one hour) and contain a list of the known responses. Responses to these queries go to the multicast address so that they can be registered by all interested computers. To keep the list up-to-date without reducing the interval, new computers use unsolicited responses when they arrive in a network to indicate there presence. Every response contains a lifetime and just before this lifetime expires the computer asks again for a response. If a computer notices that one of its responses is invalid (for instance because it is going to shut down) it sends a goodbye message which is an unsolicited response with a lifetime of zero.

A computer does the following to claim a name in *mDNS*:

1. The computer chooses a name for its IP address.
2. The computer asks three times, with a 250 ms idle time between requests, whether the name is already in use.
3. a) If there is a response within 750 ms it goes back to step 1 (and possibly sends a message to the user interface).

    b) If two computers claim the same name at the same time, there is a procedure to resolve this conflict.

    c) If there is no answer, the computer starts to claim the name with unsolicited responses. Its neighbors will replace all information regarding this name with the new information.
4. A computer must recognize conflicts at any time and be able to send *mDNS* messages, not only in the probing phase.

## DNS Service Discovery (DNS-SD)

With the first two components we can determine an IP address and a unique name in the network without explicit configuration. However it is better to be able to choose the service I need at the time from a list of services. IP addresses are established when a computer connects to the network and they change often. The names are usually controlled by the user and are relatively permanent. But the services I am interested in can be found with *DNS-SD*.

If *DNS-SD* uses *mDNS*, the same rules for conflict resolution apply. Services are advertised under the subdomains _tcp and _udp (for example: Internet Printing Protocol '_ipp._tcp.local). There was a free registry for services till 2010 at www.dns-sd.org[6] but now these services may be registered directly with IANA.

Because there may be different protocols for the same service - for instance UNIX LPR (_printer._tcp), IPP (_ipp._tcp), tcp connections to port 9100 (_pdl-datastream._tcp), remote USB emulations (_riousbprint._tcp) for printer services - one of these protocols is called the flagship protocol. Any computer that wants to register one of these protocols with *mDNS* must also register the flagship protocol so that the *mDNS* conflict resolution can work if two computer try to register two different print services with the same name. If one computer does not use the flagship protocol, it sets its port to 0 to make it clear that the name is claimed but that this protocol is not in service.

DNS-SD TXT records allow more information to be provided that is not otherwise available with the protocol.

DNS Service Discovery may use standard DNS and - using this - extend beyond the limit of the local network.

Within Linux the Avahi Framework provides appropriate soft-

---

[6]http://www.dns-sd.org/ServiceTypes.html

ware for Zero Configuration Networking. I can find Zeroconf extensions for other software, for instance the apache webserver, on Debian-derived distributions using `apt-cache search zeroconf`.

# Glossary

**BIOS**
: the **Basic Input/Output System** is the firmware on X86 computers. It is written to the ROM on the main board of the computer and is launched immediately after the computer is switched on. It is responsible for initializing the hardware, if required, and for loading the operating system using a boot loader. Parts of the BIOS may be stored on peripheral devices like network interface cards or hard disk adapters.

**Boot loader**
: a small program which is loaded and executed by a computer's firmware. It is responsible for loading and starting the operating system.

**BSD** **Berkeley Software Distribution** is a version of UNIX which was created at the University of California Berkeley. Originally BSD was based on AT&T sources, but later it was rewritten so that now there is no line of AT&T's source code in the current BSD sources and its derivatives. BSD is one of the two main lines of UNIX development along with *System V*.

**BSD license**
: the license of Berkeley Software Distribution stands for a group of Open Source licenses. Software distributed under this license may be used, adapted and distributed freely.

The only condition is that the copyright notice may not be removed. In contrast to the GPL, derived software may be distributed under other licenses.

**CD-ROM**
**Compact Disk Read Only Memory** is the compact disk's second application after the Audio CD. CD-ROMs are used to install operating systems, for live systems, for software and data distribution and for archiving.

**CF, CompactFlash**
is an interface standard for memory media. In addition to the memory chips, CF cards contain a controller that manages the memory inside the CF card and provides the computer with an IDE interface.

**Chain loading**
If a bootloader loads and executes another bootloader from another partition, this is called chain loading. Here a bootloader with a boot menu may be executed first followed by the loading and execution of the second boot loader in accordance with the selected operating system. This is a method for using several different operating systems on the same computer in a multi-boot system.

**CLI** The **command line interface** allows a software or operating system to be controlled in text mode.

**CMOS**
**Complementary Metal Oxide Semiconductor** is the name of a group of low-power semiconductors. Unlike TTL circuits the typical operating voltage is between 0.75 and 15 volts. The inputs of CMOS circuits are sensitive to

electrostatic discharge and excess voltage and should be protected by an appropriate circuitry.

CPU the **Central Processing Unit** is the part of the computer which executes the instructions of a program.

**DHCP**
**Dynamic Host Configuration Protocol** enables the server to carry out network configuration for a client computer. There is more information about this protocol in chapter 10.

**DMA**
**Direct Memory Access** means peripheral devices are able to directly access the main memory of a computer. Usually all of the memory is controlled by the CPU. All memory access utilizes the CPU which means there is a high workload with data intensive input/output. On the other hand the CPU may become bottlenecked and slow down the entire computer. DMA enables some peripherals, for instance network interface cards, hard disk adapters or USB host controllers, to exchange data with the memory without using the CPU.

DNS the **Domain Name System** is a global directory that manages the internet's name space. RFC1034 and RFC1035 describe the basic principle of the DNS.

**File system**
a file system denotes the organization of the deposition of files on the data storage media of a computer. A file is the general term for a sequence of octets (bytes) which is either stored as is on a data medium or simulated by

an input/output device. There are different file systems for storing files on data media which are geared to the requirements and capabilities of the operating system.

**GNU**

**GNU's Not UNIX** is a recursive acronym which is the name of a project whose goal is to develop a fully free operating system. Because nearly everything except the kernel was usable when Linux first appeared, a large part of a Linux system usually consists of GNU software. Therefore many people talk about GNU/Linux systems. The software license GPL is closely connected to the GNU project.

**GPIO**

**General Purpose Input/Output** is the name for input and output lines of computer chips whose behavior can be determined by software.

**GPL** the **General Public License** is a license published by the *Free Software Foundation* which originated from the *GNU* project. The basic principle of the GPL is that all software which is derived from software under the GPL may only be distributed under the same conditions (i.e. under the GPL). This principle can be found in some other licenses but it conflicts with the *BSD license* which allows software to be distributed under any conditions.

**HTTP**

**Hypertext Transfer Protocol** is the protocol which became dominant with the world wide web. It is implemented in every web browser and web server and is increasingly being used for other data transfer purposes. In principle this protocol is stateless. When using this protocol in a session containing multiple data transfers, the application must store the state itself.

ICMP
: **Internet Control Message Protocol** is an auxiliary protocol to the Internet Protocol which is used to send control messages regarding data transfer.

I²C
: the **Inter-Integrated Circuit** bus is a serial data bus developed by Philips Semiconductors which uses two lines. It is mainly used for communication between different device parts, for instance between a controller and peripheral sensors.

  Some manufacturers call the I²C bus "Two-Wire Interface" (TWI). Technically I²C and TWI are identical.

IDE
: **Integrated Device Electronics** denotes another data bus for peripheral devices.

IETF
: the **Internet Engineering Task Force** is an organization which is concerned with the technical evolution of the Internet.

IPv4
: **Internet Protocol Version 4** is currently the basis of a large part of the internet. It is used to connect computers in arbitrary networks and relies on unique addresses. Its 32-bit addresses mean there are only 4,294,967,296 unique addresses possible. In 2011 the last free IPv4 addresses were given to the ISPs (Internet Service Providers). Through

various technologies, like NAT or port-based addressing, the assignment of these last addresses has been postponed for as long as possible. Meanwhile a changeover to IPv6 is becoming increasingly urgent.

IPv6 **Internet Protocol Version 6** is the designated successor of IPv4. With its 128-bit addresses it allows for far more addresses than its predecessor and, even at its inception in the 1990s, offered many new features over the IPv4, like IPSEC and stateless auto-configuration. Many of these features where adapted to the IPv4. The adoption of IPv6 has been slow due to the delay in assigning the last IPv4 addresses.

JFFS2
**Journalling Flash File System version** 2 is a log-based file system for direct use on flash memory. OpenWrt uses it among others things. Because ALIX devices use CompactFlash cards with their own controller, they do not require this file system.

**Kernel**
the kernel is the central part of an operating system. It is responsible for managing resources like memory, input/output devices and CPU time. It forms the lowest layer of the operating system and has direct access to the hardware.

LED **Light Emitting Diode**, a semiconductor that can glow.

**Live system**
an operating system that can be launched without installation and which doesn't change the content of the hard

disk. Usually it is installed on a CD-ROM or a USB stick and is launched from there by the BIOS.

**MAC address**
the **Media Access Control** address is an address that is unique to every network interface. It allows a device in the network to be unambiguously identified. It is related to the data link layer (layer 2) of the OSI model and is needed if one wants to explicitly address a certain device in this layer. Every host or gateway in a network needs a MAC address. Hubs and switches only need a MAC address if they are administrated from inside the network.

**MBR**
the **Master Boot Record** is the first memory block on a hard disk of X86-based computers (PCs). It contains a partition table which describes the layout of the partitions on the hard disk and optionally a bootloader which can load the operating system.

**MSS** the **Maximum Segment Size** is a parameter of the TCP protocol which determines the maximum size of the datagrams that a computer can receive. It is transmitted when the connection is established.

**MTU**
the **Maximum Transmission Unit** is the maximum size of a datagram which can be sent in a network. The MTU is 1500 Byte for ethernet and larger for gigabit ethernet. The MTU is smaller for PPPoE which is used for DSL connections.

**NAT** **Network Address Translation** is a method for hiding the addresses of a network. There are different NAT techniques with different uses. The most common is also known as *masquerading* and means that all computers in a network are externally represented by the address of the router connecting the network with other networks. This can be found in most home routers where the ISP provides the router with only one address to use on the internet.

NBP   the **Network Bootstrap Program** is a bootloader which is copied from a server via the network and executed on the computer being started. This program is responsible for loading and launching the operating system.

NTP   **Network Time Protocol** is a standard protocol for synchronizing clocks in a network. RFC5905 describes the protocol's current Version 4.

**Operating system**
the software which provides basic functions to run a computer. The operating system manages resources like memory, input and output devices, and CPU time, and schedules the execution of other programs.

**OSI model**
the **Open Systems Interconnection Reference Model** is a layered model of the International Organization for Standardization (ISO). It was developed as a design basis for communication protocols.

In this model the communication tasks are divided into seven layers in ascending order: physical, data link, network, transport, session, presentation and application. Each higher layer uses the services of the lower layers to perform its tasks.

The OSI model is only a reference or design basis. Real protocols often cover more than one layer of the OSI model. The ethernet protocol, for instance, describes layers 1 (physical) and 2 (data link).

**Path-MTU, PMTU**
: is the smallest MTU of all of the networks on the path that the datagrams use to travel between two computers. This value is important to be able to send the biggest possible datagrams that do not need to be fragmented. The PMTU can be determined automatically. For this to work it is important that certain ICMP messages reach the sender of the datagrams.

**PCI** the **Peripheral Component Interconnect** bus is a standard for connecting peripheral devices with the process chip set. The ALIX devices contain a *miniPCI* bus, a smaller variant for 32 bit which is often used in notebook computers.

**PS/2** is a serial interface used to connect a keyboard and mouse to a computer.

**PXE** the **Preboot Execution Environment** is a technique that enable computers to load the operating system using a network. This means the computer is not dependent on the mass media and operating systems installed on them. The PXE code is often located in the BIOS of the network interface card and allows the computer to communicate with DHCP and TFTP servers.

**RAM**
: **Random Access Memory** is primarily used as the main or working memory in a computer. RAM only works as a temporary storage because the processing of the data takes place in the CPU registers and permanent storage is on the file system (usually on a hard disk). There are also file systems in the RAM for temporary files which are only used during the runtime of the computer.

**RFC**
: **Request For Comment** is the name for thousands of technical and organizational documents pertaining to the Internet. With the first publication still put up for discussion, RFCs keep their names even when they have become a standard through common acceptance and usage. Some of the RFCs relevant for ALIX projects are presented in the chapter on further information. The RFC process for publishing an RFC is itself documented in RFC 2026

**ROM**
: **Read Only Memory** is storage which can't be written in normal operating mode.

**SNMP**
: the IETF developed the **Simple Network Management Protocol** to monitor and control simple network devices.

**SSH**
: **Secure Shell** is the name of the protocol and the program which you can use to make an encrypted connection to another computer. Often the remote command line is placed on your computer to call up programs on the other computer. You can also tunnel connections to the other computer which can be used by other programs to securely communicate using the SSH connection.

**System V**
: is the name of a version of the UNIX operating system from AT&T as well as the name for a class of unixoid operating systems which, unlike the BSD line, were derived from the AT&T line of UNIX.

**TCP** **Transmission Control Protocol** is a reliable, connection-orientated protocol that uses Internet Protocol. It guarantees that the data is transferred in its entirety and in the correct order as long as the connection does not break off completely.

**TFTP**
: **Trivial File Transfer Protocol** is a very simple protocol for file transferring. You can find more information on this protocol in the chapter on protocols and mechanisms.

**UBIFS**
: the **Unsorted Block Image File System** is a successor of the *JFFFS2* and a competitor of the *LogFS*. It is a file system that is used directly on flash memory. Because ALIX devices use CF cards which contain their own controller, we do not need this file system.

**UCI** OpenWrt's **Unified Configuration Interface** centralizes the configuration of installed software. Instead of configuring various files using different syntaxes you can use the command line program *uci*, which has a common syntax for all software components, to configure the software.

**UDP** **User Datagram Protocol** is a simple connectionless network protocol which uses Internet Protocol. UDP doesn't guarantee anything but it saves the effort of having to establish a connection and therefore offers advantages when transferring small volumes of data.

**UNIX**
UNIX is a multiuser operating system which was originally developed at AT&T's Bell Labs to support software development. Initially freely available, it was distributed under a proprietary license starting 1981 and again under a free license starting 2005. There have been many operating systems that have been derived from UNIX and newly written operating systems which implement the typical system functions of UNIX (POSIX). These are also called unixoid operating systems.

**UPS** **Uninterruptible Power Supply** is used to keep a computer running even in the event of a power outage. Depending on the size of the UPS it can keep the computer running for a few minutes to several hours or days. A simple UPS for ALIX computers, which you may build yourself, is outlined in the chapter about additional hardware.

**USB** the **Universal Serial Bus** is a serial bus system used to connect a computer with external devices. Devices equipped with USB can be connected and disconnected while running.

**UUID**
the **Universally Unique Identifier** is an id that is formed according to a given standard which uniquely identifies information in distributed systems without central control. RFC4122 describes the structure and namespace for UUIDs.

**VGA**
: **Video Graphics Array** is an analog standard for video transmission. The computer screen is connected to the VGA interface.

**VPN** a **Virtual Private Network** is a direct connection from one network to another network regardless of how far or near the other network is. VPNs traversing the internet are usually encrypted, but unencrypted VPNs are possible too.

**X86** is the name of a microprocessor architecture and the instruction sets used by this which was mainly developed by Intel. There are various manufacturers that build CPUs which are compatible with this architecture. The AMD Geode processors built into ALIX devices are compatible with X86.

**Zero Configuration Networking**
: combines several protocols and methods which allow computers without explicit configuration to connect and exchange data. The chapter on protocols and mechanisms goes into detail about this.

# Additional resources

## Internet

The internet usually provides information faster than books and magazines if there is a connection to it at hand. But there is still a level of uncertainty. Perhaps a website is no longer available or the operator has restructured its site and the linked content is now available through a different URL.

Sometimes I can find the page in question in the Internet Archive, the so-called Wayback Machine[7]. Unfortunately this site doesn't store all of the web pages.

Therefore this book has an accompanying web page that contains some material used in this book and a list of web links. You can find this page at:

[http://buecher.mamawe.net/books/headless-linux-en/]

## Bootloader

**lilo.alioth.debian.org**[8]
    is the homepage for the LILO bootloader.

**www.gnu.org/software/grub**[9]
    is the homepage of the GRUB bootloader.

---

[7] http://web.archive.org/

# Additional resources

www.syslinux.org[10]
: is the homepage of the SYSLINUX project.

  Most distributions provide SYSLINUX as a software package. Often you can find the documentation in the directory */usr/share/doc/syslinux/*. The most interesting files have the suffix *.txt* (pxelinux.txt, syslinux.txt, ...).

## PXE boot

www.pix.net/software/pxeboot/archive/pxespec.pdf[11]
: Preboot Execution Environment (PXE) Specification Version 2.1 is the specification for PXE published by Intel in 1999.

RFC3679[12]
: contains DHCP options that are used with PXE.

## File systems

www.7-zip.org[13]
: is the homepage of the file archiver *7-Zip*. Normally this has nothing to do with file systems, but this archiver is able to read *SquashFS* using an MS Windows computer.

---

[8] http://lilo.alioth.debian.org/
[9] http://www.gnu.org/software/grub/
[10] http://www.syslinux.org/
[11] http://www.pix.net/software/pxeboot/archive/pxespec.pdf
[12] http://tools.ietf.org/html/rfc3679

**squashfs.sourceforge.net**[14]
> the homepage for *SquashFS*.

**www.squashfs-lzma.org**[15]
> SquashFS with *LZMA* compression. This is used, among other things, in the *SLAX* project.

## ALIX hardware

**www.twam.info/hardware/alix/leds-on-alix3d3**[16]
> this article contains details about using the LEDs on ALIX boards.

**www.twam.info/.../alix/temperature-sensor-on-alix3d3**[17]
> this article goes into detail about using the temperature sensors on ALIX devices.

**www.lm-sensors.org**[18]
> the homepage of the *lm-sensors* project.

## Additional hardware

**1wt.eu/articles/alix-rtc**[19]
> *How to add a capacitor to keep RTC running on PC Engines ALIX*

---

[13] http://www.7-zip.org
[14] http://squashfs.sourceforge.net/
[15] http://www.squashfs-lzma.org/
[16] http://www.twam.info/hardware/alix/leds-on-alix3d3
[17] http://www.twam.info/hardware/alix/temperature-sensor-on-alix3d3
[18] http://www.lm-sensors.org

168                                    Additional resources

> An article by Willy Tarreau about how to keep the real time clock running on a switched-off ALIX device using a large capacitor instead of a battery.

**1wt.eu/articles/alix-ups**[20]
> *How to build a cheap UPS for PC Engines ALIX*
>
> An article by Willy Tarreau about how to build a simple and inexpensive UPS for an ALIX computer. This article inspired me to create an extended UPS circuit with signaling in the chapter on additional hardware.

**www.twam.info/...ng-additional-i2c-sensors-to-alix3d3**[21]
> Tobias Müller writes in this blog entry about connecting further sensors to the I²C bus.

**www.lm-sensors.org/wiki/i2cToolsDocumentation**[22]
> the documentation for the *i2c-tools* on the *lm-sensors* project's website.

# Linux

**buildroot.uclibc.org**[23]
> *Buildroot: making Embedded Linux easy*
>
> The homepage of the *Buildroot* project which helps to create complete embedded Linux systems.

---

[19] http://1wt.eu/articles/alix-rtc
[20] http://1wt.eu/articles/alix-ups
[21] http://www.twam.info/hardware/alix/adding-additional-i2c-sensors-to-alix3d3
[22] http://www.lm-sensors.org/wiki/i2cToolsDocumentation

**wiki.linz.funkfeuer.at/funkfeuer/HowTo/AlixBoards**[24]
: (German) this page contains a lot of useful information about ALIX boards and Linux.

**www.tldp.org/HOWTO/IO-Port-Programming.html**[25]
: the *Linux I/O port programming mini-HOWTO* from Riku Saikkonen, written in 2000 but still useful as an introduction to programming I/O-Ports for Linux.

**www.debian.org**[26]
: the homepage for *Debian GNU/Linux*

**bugs.debian.org**[27]
: the Debian Project's bugs database. If you find information about a bug number in Debian, you can append the number to this URL to find the entry. Otherwise you can search for bugs using the start page.

**kernel-handbook.alioth.debian.org**[28]
: the *Debian Linux Kernel Handbook* answers many questions regarding the compilation of the Linux kernel using Debian GNU/Linux.

**wiki.debian.org**[29]
: the Debian wiki.

You can find many interesting articles here about various aspects of this distribution. For instance:

- HowToPackageForDebian[30] an introductory article about the art of creating software packages for Debian.

www.imedialinux.com[31]
: the homepage of *iMedia Embedded Linux*.

forums.imedialinux.com/index.php?topic=49.0[32]
: *Alix3c3 USB CD-Rom Install ... How do you boot???*
  This forum thread explains how to install *iMedia Linux* from a USB CD-ROM drive. To do this a minimal system is loaded from the CF card which accesses the CD-ROM drive and starts the installation process.

www.linuxfromscratch.org[33]
: *Linux From Scratch* (LFS) is not a distribution but instead a project which provides step-by-step instructions on building your own customized Linux system directly from the sources.

openwrt.org[34]
: the homepage of the OpenWrt project which supports among other hardware ALIX devices starting from the *Kamikaze* version.

wiki.openwrt.org[35]
: this is the place to go for questions concerning OpenWrt. Under the menu entry *Documentation* you can find information on various aspects of this distribution.

forum.openwrt.org[36]
: OpenWrt forums provide help with questions that can't be answered using the documentation.

wiki.openwrt.org/doc/uci[37]
: this page contains the documentation about OpenWrt's *Unified Configuration Interface* (UCI).

www.slax.org[38]
: *Slax - your pocket operating system*

Using Slax you can assemble small graphical Linux systems which can boot from CD-ROM or USB.

www.linux-live.org[39]
: *Linux Live scripts*

This is a companion website for Slax containing scripts for Live Linux systems.

linux.voyage.hk[40]
: the homepage of *Voyage Linux*, a derivative of Debian GNU/Linux which works best on X86 embedded platforms.

www.mail-archive.com/voyage-linux@.../msg02535.html[41]
: in this posting Jeff R. Allen announced *jra-initrd* on the mailing list *[voyage-linux]* and explained its usage.

nella.org/jra/geek/jra-initrd[42]
: the download address for *jra-initrd*.

---

[23] http://buildroot.uclibc.org/
[24] https://wiki.linz.funkfeuer.at/funkfeuer/HowTo/AlixBoards
[25] http://www.tldp.org/HOWTO/IO-Port-Programming.html
[26] http://www.debian.org/
[27] http://bugs.debian.org/
[28] http://kernel-handbook.alioth.debian.org
[29] http://wiki.debian.org/
[30] http://wiki.debian.org/HowToPackageForDebian
[31] http://www.imedialinux.com/
[32] http://forums.imedialinux.com/index.php?topic=49.0
[33] http://www.linuxfromscratch.org/

## Compiling software yourself

GNU Build System[43]
: Wikipedia's page about the *GNU Build System* provides an introduction with hints and links that allow you to go more in-depth.

# Literature

**Cheshire, Stuart and Steinberg, Daniel H.; Zero Configuration Networking;**
: O'Reilly Media, 2006, ISBN 0-596-10100-7

**Sloan, Joe; Network Troubleshooting Tools;**
: O'Reilly & Associates, 2001, ISBN 0-596-00186-X

# RFC - Requests for Comment

RFCs form the basis of Internet standards. Traditionally they are published by the Internet Engineering Task Force.

---

[34] https://openwrt.org/
[35] http://wiki.openwrt.org/
[36] http://forum.openwrt.org/
[37] http://wiki.openwrt.org/doc/uci
[38] http://www.slax.org/
[39] http://www.linux-live.org/
[40] http://linux.voyage.hk/
[41] http://www.mail-archive.com/voyage-linux@list.voyage.hk/msg02535.html
[42] http://nella.org/jra/geek/jra-initrd
[43] http://de.wikipedia.org/wiki/GNU_Build_System

You can find a directory of RFCs under tools.ietf.org[44].

The official website for RFCs is the RFC editor[45].

**RFC 826**

*An Ethernet Address Resolution Protocol – or – Converting Network Protocol Addresses*

Using this protocol, internet addresses (IP) are mapped to ethernet addresses.

**RFC 1034**

*DOMAIN NAMES - CONCEPTS AND FACILITIES*

an introduction to the DNS.

**RFC 1035**

*DOMAIN NAMES - IMPLEMENTATION AND SPECIFICATION*

details about the implementation of DNS.

**RFC 1350**

*THE TFTP PROTOCOL (REVISION 2)*

describes the principal courses of actions in a file transfer using TFTP.

**RFC 2131**

*Dynamic Host Configuration Protocol*

describes DHCP for IPv4.

---

[44] http://tools.ietf.org/rfc/index
[45] http://www.rfc-editor.org/

**RFC 2347**

*TFTP Option Extension*

describes a simple extension of TFTP to negotiate options before sending the data.

**RFC 2349**

*TFTP Timeout Interval and Transfer Size Options*

describes, among other things, the *tsize* option needed by PXELINUX.

**RFC 2782**

*A DNS RR for specifying the location of services (DNS SRV)*

**RFC 3315**

*Dynamic Host Configuration Protocol for IPv6 (DHCPv6)*

**RFC 3679**

*Unused Dynamic Host Configuration Protocol (DHCP) Option Codes*

contains DHCP options which are used for PXE.

**RFC 3827**

*Dynamic Configuration of IPv4 Link-Local Addresses*

**RFC 4122**

*A Universally Unique IDentifier (UUID) URN Namespace*

describes a technique to generate UUIDs.

**RFC 4862**

*IPv6 Stateless Address Autoconfiguration*

describes in detail the automatic configuration of IPv6 addresses for hosts.

**RFC 5905**

*Network Time Protocol Version 4: Protocol and Algorithms Specification*

is the current version of the protocol which is used to synchronize the clocks of the computers in the network.

# Colophon

This book was written in the *Markdown* format with some extensions from leanpub. Then Leanpub[46] used the Markdown sources to create the PDF, EPUB and MOBI versions.

The circuit for the UPS in chapter 3 was created using *gschem* from the gEDA project and then converted to PNG.

All images were processed using the GNU Image Manipulation Program (GIMP).

The device on the cover page is an open-case ALIX 2D3 with a CompactFlash card inserted in the card drive. I used these devices to test what I wrote in this book.

---

[46]https://leanpub.com/